Black Women Speak Out!
Stories of Racial Injustice in America

ASIN: B08HXL9X8W
ISBN: 9798685774972

1st edition, September 2020
Printed in the United States of America

Dedication

We dedicate this compilation to our black ancestors whose stories were never told, and voices never heard.

Also, dedicated to every Black woman who has suffered racial injustice in America.

Table of Contents

Foreword

Listen to Black Women...
Let's be honest, since the beginning of time, Black women across the globe have been saving the people around them, and the women in this book have, in their own ways, rescued their families and communities while resiliently surviving to tell us about it. Black women bear stories of joy, hardship, triumph, community, and protective love. They are distinctive and multifaceted.

Even as I lay in my hotel room writing this, I am surrounded by my closest girlfriends in Austin, TX. I am breathing in a deep sigh of relief in recognition of the safety I feel in their presence and the gratitude I have for all that they bring into my world. These three unique, beautiful Black women have, over decades, curated a space in which I feel seen, heard, and understood. They have made a home in our friendship where cackles of laughter are the norm and where I can easily ask for my emptied cup to be filled.
It is this placemaking I want us to fully bask in.

How many times have you called an emergency happy hour with your girls to unpack a workday full of microaggressions? Or Face Timed your bestie when you got pulled over by the police to ensure you made it home safe that night?

After working with women, the last 15 years, especially Black women, I can say with confidence, this is what they do so naturally and consistently -- create space for belonging. Through their vulnerability and power, this collective of Black women authors has created yet another magical place for us to unpack the most challenging moments of racism. Through telling their own stories, they are giving us permission to boldly (and sometimes with great sadness) share our own. They are liberating us from the silence and shame that comes with being oppressed.
You will find they fought, without reserve, for causes that didn't always benefit them, and still, they chose to sacrifice more than they gained.

Through trying moments and brave choices, they have themselves become gold. They are who we are waiting for and who our world needs today. And from a deep and sincere place, they have shared the tender parts of their hearts. What a gift their voices are to us.

We must not doubt or undermine their words as the world usually does. We must believe them because in doing so, we unveil the truth no matter how uncomfortable or hard it may be. Because uncomfortable truths often invite courage within us, in reading these words and listening to their voices, we become more courageous, more resilient, and more grateful. Isn't that what we are each longing for?

I can say to you today — the great women we admire, such as Fannie Lou Hamer, Maaza Ashenafi, Shirley Chisholm, Rosa Parks, Coretta Scott King, Marian Anderson, Mary McLeod Bethune, Althea Gibson, Dorothy Height, Ida B. Wells, and Sojourner Truth (to name a few), made small and big decisions along their journeys. They decided to muster up the strength they needed to survive that day and, in doing so, helped lead their people into more liberation.

The same courage can be lived out in you too. Much like these iconic women and the friends I adore, I recognize the collective and individual lives their stories represent. While being Black is not a monolithic experience, bound to one continent, country, or type of Black, a uniting thread exists, albeit frequently missed by the rest of the world. While the journeys of sisterhood, professional aspirations, or motherhood may be our own, the far too common experiences of wrestling with the world's responses to our Blackness is indeed a shared reality.

Long before we had all the data to show us just how Black women are the most endangered group, Malcolm X clearly identified they were the most disrespected, unprotected, and neglected people among us. I believe it is each of our responsibilities to change that reality. It is also within our power to do so now. We do it by listening to the stories in books like this one.

You may find yourself reflected in their words. We are these women, and they are ultimately us. Allow their strength to be your reminder to keep going. Allow their honesty to be your breath of fresh air. Allow their vulnerability to unmask your own. Allow their words to truly seep in and heal. Whether you are a Black woman, or you are choosing to center around the voices of Black women, I implore you to read with enthusiasm and listen intently.
Thank God for Black women.

Listen to them.

Believe them.

Help heal them.

By Bemnet Meshesha

About Bemnet

Although born in Ethiopia, Bemnet lives in Dallas, Texas with her loving parents and two brothers close by. Bemnet has embraced the nuances of a hybrid identity rooted in the faith, cultures, and traditions of the two worlds she constantly vacillates between. It is from this place her passion for fairness, justice, and equity for Black people was born.

Bemnet studied at Dallas Baptist University and the University of Texas at Arlington, joining the family of social workers and community practitioners. A nonprofit professional, experienced in creating impactful programs, managing philanthropic dollars, and innovative large-scale projects, she is committed to sustainable community development. Her love for traveling, working with young people, and being a policy junkie are truly unparalleled.

Bemnet is a respected facilitator, speaker, and researcher on topics of racial equity and Black identity and experiences. Her writing can be found in national publications and academic journals like the British Journal of Social Work. Bemnet is proud of her community work, most notably her role as the first Black Immigrant President of the Dallas Ft. Worth Urban League Young Professionals and as a founding member of Heritage Giving Circle, dedicated to cultivating philanthropy among Black women. Bemnet is also a graduate of the Dana Juett Residency, a Partner at Social Venture Partners, A co-founder of Bail Out Book Club, and a fellow through the Op-Ed Project.

Introduction

America! The land of the free, the home of the brave.

The pain of black women surges throughout the corridors of this country that we call the land of the *free*. In the very place that should feel like *home*, we as women of color have faced unimaginable calamity. Surely this should classify us as---the *brave*.

Centuries of oppression have held us back while others were given a head start in life. Stumbling blocks... purposely placed in our pathways, with the sole intent of keeping us from reaching our destiny. One step forward...three steps back. We have been forced to abide by rules that were not written in our favor. At times we have felt stretched beyond our limits, like the false reach for a baton that was never meant to be passed on. While feeling as if we didn't have enough tears to cry, we have stood on the sidelines and watched the beast of racial injustice cripple our families and our communities.

Stricken, yet we stand! Bruised, yet we breathe! Restricted, yet we rise!

The idea for "Black Women Speak Out: Stories of Racial Injustice in America" was brought forth after a much needed conversation on racism between a group of black and white women called "Overcoming Racism: The Dialogue". Several of the black women experienced an awakening of emotions that were unknowingly suppressed. The white women were open to listening, educating themselves, and becoming more aware. The common thread of the dialogue seemed to be, "What can we do to help bring change?" Immediately following the conversation, the vision was released, and 25 resilient black women agreed to join us in sharing their personal experiences with racial injustice. Like proud mothers, we are elated to present to you our fascinating co-authors, of which several are even first-time writers. These women simply had a sincere desire to face and overcome their fear of writing… to share and be heard.

The current climate of our society has presented us as black women, with a golden opportunity for the muted voices attached to our wounds to be made audible. We have kept silent, far too long. Our stories are our testimonies. If the Bible speaks that we are overcome by the words of our testimony (Revelation 12:11), how will we ever reach that place of triumph if our lips remain sealed? The perfect time has arrived! We're no longer just fed up! We valiantly speak up!

This compilation of writings is one way of how we can help tear down the stubborn walls of racism. It is accurate we cannot control what happens to us, but we can control how we respond. As we have revisited hurtful places of our past (and sadly…of our present) we pray that our plight as black women is better conceived by those who may look different but have a genuine desire to know more. We pray our stories will help shed light on the darkness of racism, revealing the negative impact it has had on women of color and our families at large.

It would be unrealistic and unfair to expect everyone to fully understand how we feel or what we've endured since they have not walked in our shoes. However, we simply ask that you open your heart and mind, place yourself inside the moment, and listen with your soul, as each story is unveiled. May a new-found level of compassion be developed, and authentication of pure love generated, as the pages unfold.

Hear our stories, feel our pain, solidify our hope, as we SPEAK OUT!

Yolanda Johnson Bailey

and

Deidre Proctor

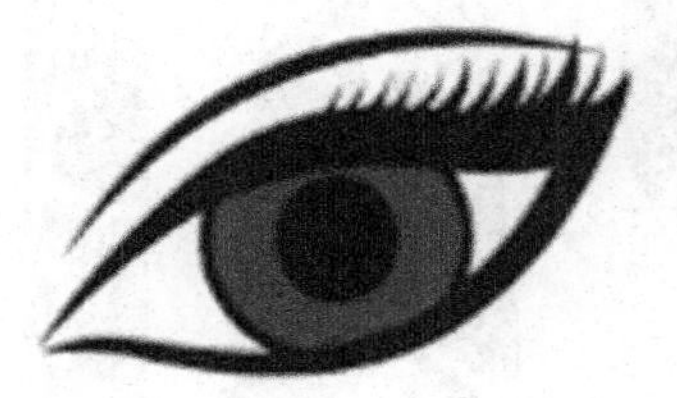

The Visionary Authors

PAIN

We come from an ancestral lineage of women who were not always allowed to vocalize their feelings or display their emotions. They were made to witness catastrophic events and violent attacks against people of color, including their own families. These heroic women carried the emotional burdens of an entire village on their shoulders. There was no such thing as family counseling or therapy sessions in their day and time. They dealt with their hurts the best way they knew how, with no time in between to heal from one blow to another.

Black women were forced to spectate the horrors of innocent bloodshed. The lives of their male kindred were ruthlessly snatched right before them. Their lips were tightly sealed as their white masters raped them, and the purity of their precious daughters stripped away. Their loving families were torn apart as they were separately sold into slavery. They fought their way through incredible mental, emotional, and physical anguish. They were the epitome of strength.

The pain from our descendants still speaks from the grave. In the year 2020, different era...same agony!

Imagine a lifetime of sobbing, crying, weeping, and moaning. If our tears were bottled up, no warehouse could accommodate them. Our hearts as black women ache for one another. We have become too familiar with this maddening thing we call pain.

Our pain is private yet public. It is silent yet loud. Numbing, yet piercing. Personal yet inclusive. It's complicated. Our pain is REAL!

Yolanda Johnson Bailey

What Racial Injustice Means To Me

“Being treated unfairly based on the color of your skin. Being limited to resources and access to capital compared to other demographics.” ~Dr. Angella Palmer-Banks~

"The act of one race feeling privileged over another." ~Marie~

"Racism blasphemes who I am! God says I am one thing, but people try to say I'm something different." ~Delisa~

“When others decide that you are not worthy to share the same benefits that they hold dear.” ~LM~

“It is the unfair, underserved, unrighteous, unwarranted, and unprovoked, or unsolicited treatment of a person because of the color of their skin. When I’m devalued and not recognized as a human being, part of God’s creation, made in His image and likeness, and I am dismissed and treated unfairly on “your” say so…another created being! Racial Injustice!” ~Veronica Sutton~

“Having a justice system that capitalizes off of the unequal rights of people of color.” ~JJ~

“People of a certain race are being subject to unjust, undeserved treatment, and outcomes, which in most cases, result in their death.” ~Carolyn Pippen~

Hear Our Voices

by Yolanda FaithEyes

Today we speak our truth
No longer fear-induced
It's time that we are heard
No mumbling of our words

Precise, explicit diction
A crystal-clear depiction
No unsubstantial chatter
On how our lives don't matter

To look upon our faces
No span of time erases
Neither hurt nor pain
Yet honor we have gained

Our blackness we are proud
Sing praises, sing out loud
Products of the family tree
Melanin in shades of three

Embrace our skin and let it be
Make peace and live in harmony
We're siblings, can't you see
God fathers you and me

Our stories shall be told
From youngest to the old
Race has been a nemesis
Flashback to the genesis

Former shackles, now we're free
Free to speak, free to be
Embrace our color, don't erase
Let's move forward to a place

Where not another day
Racism sees, we pray
Hopefully, your choice is
To frankly hear our voices

Stories

Chapter 1
"The Past Inside of the Present"

By Deidre Proctor

When Mr. George Floyd was killed by a white policeman with a dark heart in Minneapolis, Minnesota, the world's eye was finally opened and focused on America, home of the brave and land of the free. The unhidden secrets were let out. The past years, even centuries, in America include slavery, oppression, depression, death, segregation, red-lining, hate-crimes, and many other types of racism and racial injustices. The world and many White Americans are now saying "no way," "unbelievable," "is this real?", "How could they?", "How can they?", "What can I do?", and "What can we do?".

One of the awesome social media female entrepreneur groups I belong to took to the group's comment section and filled it with those questions and more. They also asked to be educated on how their businesses can be more diverse and inclusive. Other Black women in the predominately white group offered comments that were so beautiful and articulated so well. So, I had the bright idea that I would also write a "deep" post about racism in America.

As I sat down to begin typing in that comment section, my mind went back, way back, to my childhood. I started thinking about moments with my parents that I had not thought of in years. Then I began thinking about my children's childhood. Suddenly, I couldn't type, my eyes filled with tears, and I had an overwhelming feeling of sadness as I re-lived those times. Allow me to share three of those memories with you.

Memory #1

My parents were born in the South. My mother was born in Tennessee, and my dad was born in Mississippi. After they married, they settled down in Tennessee. My mother's father had previously traveled up north and found a home and job in Indiana. He contacted my mother and told her that if they moved to Indiana, he guaranteed a job for my dad. So, they moved, dad got a job in the Steel Mills, and they started their life in the north.

Since my dad's parents still lived in Mississippi, we traveled back every summer to visit them. As a little girl in the '60s, I loved those trips. I knew I would get to see Big Momma and Big Daddy, along with my cousins, aunts, and uncles. But my favorite part of the trip was the food my mother would pack for us to take on that 10-hour trip. I could not wait to eat her fried chicken. It was the best! We never stopped at restaurants along the way, which was not strange to me because we had all that delicious food Momma packed. We had so much food and water that Dad didn't even go inside the gas stations to buy goodies after he paid the gas attendant.

It was not until I was much older that I found out the reason we did not stop at any food stops along the highway or go into the gas stations. It was because we were not allowed. Those establishments did not allow "colored people" to enter into their facilities. My parents never spoke about racism in our home. It was simply the way of life for them. They never explained to me why we never ate at those restaurants. It was almost like, don't talk about it and it goes away. Like Santa Claus or the Easter Bunny, if you don't tell the child they aren't' real, they will eventually figure it out on their own.

When I reflected on this memory, I thought how horrible that my father, a great man, was treated like he was an infected animal. My mother had to witness and adapt to this way of life from birth until adulthood. My mother was one of the most giving persons I have ever known. My dad always had a pleasant attitude and a ready smile. He was a rock for everyone he met. Quiet, but ready to lend a hand or hearty laugh. And yet, these "people" treated him like trash to take out.

As I looked in the mirror, I screamed in my head, "BUT WE ARE HUMAN! I AM HUMAN!" The tears started flowing…

Memory #2

When I started reflecting on those trips, I remember whenever we had to urinate, my dad would pull over on the side of the road. I would hop out of the car, and my mother would get out with me and stand in a position so that the cars passing by could not see all of me. My dad would go deeper into the weeds to pee. When I was finished, my mom would tell me to turn around and stand there while she squatted. This was normal for me. My mom taught me how to squat and hold my panties so I would not get anything splashed on myself. I thought everyone (black and white) peed on the side of the road!

Again, it was not until I was much older that I realized why we always pulled over to the side of the road. We could not use the restrooms along the highway because we were "Colored" we were not allowed.

How could a race of people (the white race) determine their feces and urine was so special that it could not mix with ours, or that their disinfectant products would not work on Black folks' germs. What type of people conjured up such a mindset? And not just white people, but also "Christian" white folks believed we were sub-human and treated us so violently. Madness!

As I looked in the mirror, I screamed in my head, "BUT WE ARE HUMAN! I AM HUMAN!" The tears started flowing…

Memory #3

I am no longer a child, but a wife and mother. We moved to Texas and I enrolled my oldest son into kindergarten. Not too long after school started, I received a call from his white teacher. She said he was the only Afro-American child in her class, and she felt he would get bullied by the other children. So, I asked her if she was suggesting I take him out of her class, and she said yes.

What do you think I did? If you said I took my baby out of her class, you would be right. Now, I could have responded to that teacher with "You are the teacher. It is your job to stop the bullying," or I could have said, "Kids are taught to bully and very seldom have four and 5-year-old children crafted the art of bullying". However, my main concern was the safety of my child, not getting him away from the other children, but from that teacher. In fact, I enrolled him in a different school.

Instead of seeing 20 little angels in her classroom, she saw a barrel of apples with one bad apple in the bunch. Instead of seeing 20 precious minds to teach and to shape, she saw 19 "good" kids and one that had no value at all. So, she had to get rid of that one.

That One, my baby boy, grew up to be an outstanding man. One of his paintings was hung in the State capital; he has a bachelor's degree in Finance and a bachelor's degree in Accounting, has played professional volleyball overseas and coached outstanding players. An awesome husband, great father, and the little black kindergartner that his white teacher kicked out.

As I looked in the mirror, I screamed in my head, "BUT WE ARE HUMAN! I AM HUMAN!" The tears started flowing…

As the memories kept coming mixed with the current events, I realized that the racial injustice to Black people in America today is no different than the past injustices Black people suffered in the past. The dates are different, but the hatred for Black people exists today. The methods of torment are different, but the torments yet exist today. The cruel people of the past have died, but their legacy lives on in their families. The suffering my parents, grandparents, great-grandparents, and great-great-grandparents endured will be compared to the suffering that I, my children, grandchildren, and great-grandchildren endures and will endure.

Black people are so very tired of the repulsive, horrendous, inexcusable, and dreadful ways we are treated; however, we are not surprised by it. That in itself is so sad. The current state of America's love for all of its people is no closer today than it was yesterday. Why? Because too many White Americans are in a state of denial, which is why racism flourishes.

I do want to include in my story that I am so blessed to have met and personally know white men and women who are not in denial and who truly have a love for black people, all people. They may not have our experiences, but they do acknowledge our pain. When I cry, they cry. They are in the forefront fighting for justice for all. To those, I salute you! There is simply not enough of them…yet.

Yes, we are all human. We are all sons and daughters of God. But sometime after leaving the Garden, we lost our way. We developed caste systems, classes of people, division, separations, different values, different principles, different beliefs, racism, racial and social injustices. Instead of love for all, some people choose who they will love and who they do not have to love. Those people then fixed their minds that God was fine with that. NEWS FLASH: He is not!

I want to share the following two scriptures with you:

"A new command I give you: Love one another. As I have loved you, so you must love one another." John 13:34-35

“Love your neighbor as yourself. There is no commandment greater than these." Mark 12:31

It is my hope that one day, the fears and hurts that Black women and all Black people endure in America will be a thing of the past. I know this is possible because God said, *“if my people, who are called by my name, will humble themselves and pray and seek my face and turn from their wicked ways, then I will hear from heaven, and I will forgive their sin and will heal their land.”* 2 Chronicles 7:14

Let the healing begin…

About Deidre

Deidre Proctor, Certified Clarity and Accountability Coach, is the CEO of Deidre Proctor & Associates, LLC. She is also an Author, Speaker, Philanthropist, Mentor, and Ministry Leader.

With over 20 years of experience in sales, marketing/sales training, and strategy development, Deidre's passion for helping others to achieve their goals has made her a highly sought-after Business Coach and Mentor to women who desire clarity in finding their purpose and those who have goals of starting their own business. She also created the **Personal Passion Signature Program** for Female Entrepreneurs. Deidre realized early on that she best fulfills her destiny when she helps others grow.

She is the Co-Founder and CEO of **Amazing Retreats International, LLC.** With the support of her husband, David, she plans and hosts amazing retreats that leave the attendees with ah-ha moments every time. From Women retreats, to family retreats, to couples' retreats, to business retreats, she plans each one with her heart and gives attention to the smallest details.

Through their annual signature retreat, The **Breathe Retreat**, she has brought together Christian women from all walks of life that simply need a break from the hustle and bustle of life. This retreat is only for women who are ready to be refreshed, refocused, and rejuvenated with no distractions from home life or work life. The Breathe Retreat has sold out since its 2015 conception, praise God!

Deidre is also the Founder and CEO of **SHARE YOUR GENIUS**. SYG is a group of businesswomen, entrepreneurs, and Ministry Leaders (current, retired, or aspiring), that support each other by sharing the unique skills and talents God has equipped us with. This support includes clarity, mindset, inspiration, empowerment, strategy, and accountability. www.shareyourgenius.org

Deidre has been featured in media platforms such as Voyage Dallas Magazine, Xcellence Magazine, Heart and Soul Magazine, Girlfriends Gathering Magazine, North Dallas Gazette, Lavida News/The Black Voice, and is a sought-after guest at various seminars and radio stations.

She is the author of the Clarity To Success Journal and Co-Author of Black Women Speak Out: Stories of Racial Injustice in American.

Deidre loves reading and taking road trips with her husband. She is a Wife, Mother, and Grandmother. Deidre and her husband reside in Texas. For more information, or to contact Deidre, please visit: https://www.deidreproctorassociates.com

Chapter 2
"My Race Journey…*to be Continued*"

by Dr. La Tonya Woodson-Mayfield

"I press toward the mark for the prize of the high calling of God in Christ Jesus" Philippians 3:14 KJV

"You can be anything you want to be" is a phrase we often heard from our parents while growing up. The same sentiments were shared by our teachers and church leaders, all adding that if we stayed in school, worked hard, and obeyed those in authority, we'd somehow make it on the other side of the railroad, the greener pastures, so to speak. There was a sense from our parents and leaders that they wanted our generation, those of us born almost two decades after the Vietnam War and the Hippie era, to be better than them. They didn't want us to experience the devastating racial injustices of what they experienced as children in the 50s and 60s, and even what their brothers experienced after returning home from the war. They desired for us to achieve the next level of success in both life and career.

Some of our parents would work two and three jobs and make huge sacrifices for us in an attempt to shield us from America's systemic injustices that seemed to influence every single area of our lives. Those major areas included housing, education, and health. Because our families, classrooms, communities and inner circles were mostly homogenous, meaning predominantly Black, there was one additional caveat that was worth mentioning to our generation at the time. That was, in order to achieve the American dream of having a full-time job and family, and owning a home with a white picket fence and two cars, you had to work twice as hard, stay in school longer, and never ever break any stated or implied laws. And even then, with your best intentions, there were no guarantees that any of our dreams would come true. As Black Americans, our dream possibilities seem to be confined to a short list of careers and neighborhoods---and self-care, particularly mental health care, was not even a consideration.

The idea of a weekly or monthly session with a counselor or therapist was taboo in our community. In fact, as always, the "systems" were systematically working overtime against us as a people. The results damaged our communities, our families, our careers, and our mental health. Thankfully, our spirit of resilience may have been bruised, but it certainly was not broken. I, for one, was determined to fight against these systems with everything in me. Here is my race journey.

I remember vividly the day I got the call from a recruiter offering me a job as a banking officer. "Wow," I thought after a shout of jubilation with my hand over the phone receiver. Just to have the word "officer" in my title made me feel like I had arrived at the C-Suite. You mean, I, the dark-skinned young black woman from the 'hood' would be the one sitting around the boardroom table, rubbing shoulders with the big boys? I imagined myself dressed in my dark suit, presenting a high-profile business report, and leading a discussion, all in a matter of seconds, during this initial reaction. I was beside myself. As the recruiter explained the position a little more in detail, I immediately returned to reality. As it turned out, the office job was an outside sales position. In reality, I'd be selling checking and savings accounts to individuals that worked for certain client companies. But, that brief moment of being in greener pastures was still lingering in my thoughts. The sales job was fun most days, and I enjoyed working with my colleagues. Plus, as a college student, working at a bank was much more appealing to me than a fast food restaurant. I worked hard and had no complaints. In fact, I was very successful in my role.

My communications background was paying off, as it allowed me to excel in customer service and exceed my sales goals. Things were going well until I started hearing from my Black friends at other branches that they were being treated unfairly. They shared on multiple occasions that they were being accused of being short with customers or not showing up to work on time. One of them even got accused of stealing money, although it was never proven. They also shared that they repeatedly were insulted or shamed and increasingly excluded from break room conversations and group events. Instead, they were the subject of those break room conversations. Although, I believed my friends' accounts, I didn't believe, at the time, that I needed to intervene other than to listen and console them. In hindsight, it was a selfish thought. Obviously, they were being targeted because they were Black and successful in their roles. One of my friends was fired, but she quit before her manager could formally give her walking papers. My other friend resigned shortly after.

Somehow, those former words of wisdom began to speak loudly to me. Now, the scrutiny was certainly going to intensify for the remaining few of us. In my gut, I knew I'd be next. Within a few days, my new manager began to challenge my decisions with no other reason than she disagreed with me or that I should have done things differently. After consistently posting superior sales and surpassing goals, even establishing new relationships that had been tried unsuccessfully by others in the past, she was still hell-bent on attacking my performance and character. When she learned that I reported her to our director, she moved full steam ahead. In one meeting, she simply explained that she did not like me.

Here I was, a young Black woman, now a recent college grad, soaring in sales and working for a same-aged, non-degreed White woman. I, like my former Black colleagues, was a threat to her and those others like her throughout the company. We were four twenty-something years old, educated Black women who were excelling in our respective areas, yet confined to our entry-level roles, reporting to White women that rose through the ranks because of their small town, legacy networks. That was the corporate culture, the unwritten law of the company. We certainly could not violate that law.

After a night of tossing and turning and literally feeling sick to my stomach, I woke up the next morning for work, got dressed, and prepared for the worse. I remember sharing with my close friend at work that something felt weird about that day, and I specifically loosely detailed how I thought the day would end. I quickly gathered my personal belongings, which weren't many, and just waited. I was called into my manager's office about an hour later. She told me that my work was no longer needed. I paused for a few seconds, smiled, and simply said, "Thank you and God bless you." I vowed that from that day on, I would never keep silent when there is injustice, even a whisper of it. Racism in the workplace is real. It hurts deeply. It crushes confidence. It shatters goals and dreams.

I can honestly name dozens of friends, colleagues, and acquaintances that have shared their race stories with me. It's the focus of many of our conversations when we're in our safe places. Being overlooked for projects, training new colleagues for roles that we should have been promoted to, being subjected to unwarranted scrutiny or the countless microaggressions that we experience daily, all day long, are just a few of the matters of workplace racism that we talk about. It's cemented and permeates throughout many companies and because Black people have so much at risk if we complain or just raise it as a concern, workplace racism never gets fully dealt with. Instead, we are labeled as the antagonists and always throwing out the race card. No matter how hard we try as Black women, over and over and over again, we keep getting pushed back.

According to McKinsey research, "Black women face the greatest barriers to progress in the workplace, a consequence of accumulation of different forms of discrimination, including racism, sexism, and classism." The systems are designed to interrogate us, intimidate us, and strip us of our confidence. Yet, we keep fighting.

My race journey continues. Fighting racial injustice is a personal conviction for me. It's why I first ran for public office in 2017 and thankfully won. I use my voice and my platform to speak on equity in education for all students. Fighting racial injustice is why I carefully consider the social, community, and civic boards I join. Their values have to align with mine in that there is no room or tolerance for racial injustice or inequities. It's why I continue educating myself on race and cultures and those resources that help me understand how to combat various types of injustice. It's also why I continue to stay grounded in the word of God as my guide and moral compass. My faith in God has never wavered. The physical toil and emotional trauma of racism have certainly been exhausting. But, I'm too sick and tired of being sick and tired and feeling too powerless to do anything to help support the cause.

I've always had an appreciation for people's differences, even when those differences often conflicted with my thoughts and approaches to various situations. We all have varying styles of communication, leadership, personality, and other areas, not to mention that our backgrounds and experiences help shape our beliefs and values. In the workplace, I greatly appreciate the diversity of thoughts and perspectives, no matter who's sharing them. I'm thankful that I can sit at the boardroom table with executives or the breakroom table with colleagues or sit in my office or cubicle with anyone who visits and learn from and contribute to meaningful and enriching conversations.

What I refuse to have tolerance for is racism, including racism in the workplace, which has been the silent, but pervasive enemy for far too long. My work in diversity and inclusion allows me to be a resource for underrepresented candidates, as well as a consultant to companies committed to shifting cultural paradigms and becoming inclusive for all employees. This work is my personal mission.

For anyone that experiences racism in the workplace, consider raising your voice of concern via whatever resources are available to you. Being silent is not an option. But be prepared to offer a solution to the issue or be willing to share your expectations for a positive outcome. Yes, the risk of raising your voice is great, but the risk of not speaking up and out is even greater. Commit to writing your personal race journey and propose what you want the ending to be. Press on!!

McKinsey & Company. May 19, 2020. “Diversity wins: How inclusion matters.” https://www.mckinsey.com/featured-insights/diversity-and-inclusion/diversity-wins-how-inclusion-matters#

About Dr. La Tonya

La Tonya brings over 20 years of Human Resources experience to her role as Global Diversity and Inclusion Manager at Korn Ferry International. In her previous roles, La Tonya contributed her HR expertise in the areas of Leadership Development, Organizational Development, Learning and Development, Employee Engagement, Talent Acquisition, Career Development, Employee Relations, and Executive Coaching.

A sought-after speaker, La Tonya uses her talents as a motivational/keynote speaker at seminars, retreats, and conferences. She is the co-author of Power Moms, a book of inspirational stories about the many contributions, trials, and triumphs that Mothers from all walks of life experience.

La Tonya is actively engaged in numerous member-based organizations and community/civic activities, including her church, Great Commission Baptist Church, her sorority, Alpha Kappa Alpha Sorority, Inc., and Jack and Jill of America, Inc., where she serves as an Executive Board member for the Fort Worth Chapter and as the South Central Region Legislative Chair on the National Legislative Committee. She is also a Board Member for the TCU AddRan College of Liberal Arts and a Board Member for the Multicultural Alliance of Texas. As an elected official, she serves as a Board Trustee for the Crowley Independent School District.

She is a proud graduate of the Magnet program at Polytechnic High School and received a BS in Speech Communications, with an emphasis in HR, from Texas Christian University, an MS in Human Resources Management and Training and Development from Amberton University, and a Ph.D. in Applied Training, Performance Improvement from the University of North Texas. She is also a recent Class of 2020 graduate of the prestigious Leadership Fort Worth, which promotes diversity and inclusion in the city of Fort Worth and surrounding communities.

La Tonya loves building positive relationships and encouraging individuals, no matter where they are in their educational career or life journey, to reach their optimal potential. In her spare time, she enjoys writing, volunteering, and spending quality time with her husband and two children.

Chapter 3
"The Unjust Road Back Home"

By Cassandra Y. Thomas

As I share my family's story, at this moment in time, we are in the middle of the Covid-19 pandemic and national protest sparked by the murder of George Floyd at the hands of police. Chants of "Black Lives Matter" are met with chants of "Blue Lives Matter" and "White Lives Matter." It is the resistance to acknowledge the idea that black lives are under attack and have been for decades, even centuries in one form or another. You may have heard people say how slavery and Jim Crow happened long ago, but when you look at these conditions generationally, it really wasn't that long ago.

Take my paternal grandfather, for example, a sharecropper born out of slavery but raised on a plantation in Mississippi until he and his family left to re-settle in the early 1900s. My maternal grandmother, who experienced being told at the end of her workweek, "I'm sorry, but I don't have any money to pay you today, but I have some old clothes you can take to your children." She was only being paid $4.00 per week, to begin with. These were not distant ancestors who passed long before my time. They were my beloved grandparents.

Sure, a lot has changed, and great strides have been made, but as my grandmother would say, "The good old days were not that good. She didn't like the phrase "Back in the good old days..." because during her time, she lived through a lot of injustice. I am grateful for all the sacrifices she, my parents, and many others made so that I would have a better life. On the flip side, it is not hard to recognize that there are those whose grandparents and parents who rendered those injustices still continue in their legacy.

My television is full of stories of our president sending "secret police" to break-up peaceful protesters. My neighbor, as friendly as he may be, has installed three flags across the front of his home, an American Flag, A Trump Flag, and a Blue Lives Matter Flag. When my daughters left home the other day noticing the flags, they immediately called home in shock and dismay of his display. After the world recently witnessed the horrible death of George Floyd, if all lives matter, then the American Flag at this time should be enough. It was as if he needed to waive his banner of distraction. At this time, the country has lost one of its heroes recently, Rep. John Lewis, who was beaten and trampled in Selma, Alabama marching for voter rights back in 1965. Violence against the marchers was carried out by the hands of the police. Make no mistake, I support our local police and law enforcement, but as black people, we also find ourselves being hopeful that the heart of the man wearing the uniform is one we can rely on.

The current climate reminds me of the injustice my parents experienced when they were young adults. When my parents finished school, they each journeyed to Chicago, my mom from Tennessee and my father from Louisiana, part of the Great Migration. They were leaving the south to seek better opportunities for themselves in the north. They met in a little church in the south suburbs of Chicago, married, and had me. This smart, energetic young couple secured jobs, built a home, and were set to achieve all the American dream would provide.

One Labor Day Weekend, my parents decided to take advantage of the long weekend and take a road-trip back home for the holiday. They drove to Millington, TN to visit my mother's family and then on to Louisiana to visit my father's family. It was on the latter leg of that trip that trouble was encountered. This is when they really began to understand the second set of rules that African American travelers had to navigate. On the route between Tennessee and Louisiana, my father stopped at a gas station in Mississippi to fill-up as they made their way to Louisiana. While the attendant pumped their gas, my father and my mother's cousin, who had joined the trip from Tennessee, went to the restroom. My mother stayed in the car, holding me on her lap. A couple of guys sitting in the gas station, who appeared to be attendants, went into the bathroom behind my father and cousin and proceeded to strike them with a gun. In the confines of that little gas station restroom, my father and cousin fought for their lives to escape.

My father still bears a scar on his hand from knocking one of the attackers through the back door, which allowed them to escape. They ran toward the car, and behind them followed the two white attackers determined to carry out their terror. With guns pointed in our car, the men threatened to shoot us as my father and cousin jumped in the car. My father hit the accelerator and drove off. After he had driven for nearly 30 minutes up the highway, he looked in his rear-view mirror and saw flashing lights speeding behind us. Was this help we could rely on or more danger? Ahead of us appeared to be what looked like a ball of fire. It was actually a roadblock of red flashing siren lights. My father pulled to the side of the road and was ordered out of the car. There he stood with his face and shirt covered in blood from the injuries he had just received, and now the officer tells him he is being arrested for leaving the gas station without paying for gas and disturbing the peace!

My father tried to explain to the officer what happened, but his words fell on deaf ears. He was handcuffed and put in the squad car. Fortunately, he had mapped out the directions and gone over them with my cousin and mother at the beginning of the trip. My father was driven away and my mother and cousin were left to make it to my grandparents on their own. My mother and cousin made it to the small town of Clinton and stopped for directions to my grandparent's farm. Once they explained what had happened, the parishioner quickly led them the way.

What should have been a joyful arrival was instead a panic and fear-stricken arrival. My mother hurried out of the car and rushed to my grandparents to explain what happened. My mother could literally see my grandfather's heart beating through his shirt. My grandfather, being well known in the small town of Clinton, Louisiana, took my mother and went to his sheriff's office. When they arrived at the Clinton sheriff's office and explained the ordeal, the sheriff proceeded to call over to the Mississippi sheriff and inform him, saying, "This is the Sheriff of Clinton, and you have my friend's son in your jail." As the conversation ended, the Mississippi sheriff replied, "Tell them to bring $25, and they can come to get him out." The charge was "Disturbing the Peace." Because they were from out of town, it was assumed they were in town to participate in the Civil Rights protests and boycotts, when in fact, this was nothing more than a family visit. My grandfather and mother drove to Mississippi, picked up my father, and took him straight to the hospital to get stitches and his wounds treated from the gas station ordeal. They returned home, and our family stayed there as planned.

When the time came to drive back to Chicago, fearing for their safety, they left their car and opted to return to Chicago by train. How could they not fear for their safety? They could not even trust the police would come to their aide. After a month, they did return to pick up their car. They were cautious about every move and where they stopped for gas. They packed their lunch and dinner for the road, daring not to stop for food, as most places along the route would not have served them anyway. During this time, laws in the South made it easy for African Americans to be fined or jailed for “Disturbing the Peace,” especially while the Civil Rights Protests were going on. Sound familiar? Sadly, these were the rules that my family, extended family, and many other African American families were subjected to when traveling through the South for years to come.

So many African American families have stories like these and worse. Unlike today, there were no cell phones or cameras to capture those incidents, which made reports of them easy to discount. When my parents returned to Chicago, they hired a civil rights attorney who worked on the case for about six months. In the course of the investigation, the service station changed ownership. Deception and cover-up became clear, and with no witnesses, it became a matter of my parent’s word against theirs. Ultimately, the case became too difficult and expensive to pursue.

My parents didn't let this stop them. Through prayer, perseverance, and hard work, they built successful careers and lives. It is my hope that sharing this experience in some way weakens the resistance to recognizing there are still systemic problems in this country from our past that need to be dealt with, addressed, and reconciled rather than ignored and deflected, else I fear that history will repeat itself.
All lives won't matter until black lives matter.

About Cassandra

Cassandra Thomas is currently an IT professional with over 20 years of experience in software support. She has held various roles including Technical Analyst, Senior Technical Engineer, and her current role as Principal Technical Support Engineer. Cassandra has been recognized as a Financial Controls expert at her company and a very significant contributor to the success of her global team in software support and productivity.

She earned her bachelor's degree from Chicago State University and Certification in Computer Programming from the Florida Institute of Technology.

Cassandra is committed to serving her community and her church. She and her husband of 27 years humbly serve as part of the Deacon and Deaconess Ministry, and she is a very active leader on her church's volunteer staff, utilizing her professional skills for the advancement of ministry. She has two lovely college-age daughters who are successfully matriculating at Florida A & M University.

Chapter 4
"A Challenged Promise"

By Cheylon D. Brown

Almost all the boxes are complete on my checklist! The successful navigation of community college is near. However, the main box is still not checked. Spring 1993 is my graduation semester; it presented numerous options, and I was about to keep my promise to mom. My first degree- an Associate of Arts from the local community college is almost completed. The big question remained unanswered... where would I continue my education?

Unfortunately, the murder of my mom at twelve years old still haunted me. My heart kept saying I could not go too far. I need to stay close to home in case something happened to my dad. With the help of an amazing counselor, Dr. Allen, I began to submit college applications to colleges and universities within a four-hour driving range. Other than math, my grades were good; I was involved in extra-curricular classes, so why was the fear of non-acceptance strangling me? I could hear the voices of the naysayers taunting me, and even though I had a village of diverse high school teachers coupled with one professor and one counselor/professor, the voices of the naysayers were loud. But thankfully, my village was there cheering and encouraging me every step of the way and reminding me that I had the determination and strength to complete what I had started. More so, I had an obligation to those scholarship donors. They were counting on me to keep my word and make them proud.

Then, it happened! Dr. Allen called me to her office and shared information concerning a highly selective research program that offered financial assistance to students seeking a bachelor's degree, interested in research, and determined to earn a doctorate. It was the answer I needed because the program was offered at two of the schools I was hoping to attend, and they added a new area for transfer students. The application deadline required a quick turnaround, so I quickly went to work. Dr. Allen proofread the essay and made sure I submitted it on time. After submitting the application, the waiting period seemed long. I was working, going to school, attending church, volunteering, and serving as a leader in my organization, but nothing seemed to calm my anxious spirit. The program was supposed to notify the recipients in March, but it seemed as if March was never coming. Coincidentally, college admission letters were shortly to follow. Remaining focused was difficult.

On a typical day of college, classes finished, and leadership began. The African Student Organization had a meeting in the Student Center in the afternoon. Dr. Allen, also the organization's advisor, told me to meet her at her office following the meeting. I had no idea what to expect. The meeting discussion was action-packed, and our leadership team worked. The day fulfilled its purpose.

According, immediately after the meeting, I met her at the office, and she handed me an envelope. Nervously, I opened the letter, and I remember seeing the word Congratulations… I thought to myself, oh my God, I got in. Smiling from ear to ear, I breathed deeply. Humbled, I was once again able to keep the promise to my mom. The research program provided enough stipend money along with a paid research position that university life began to resemble a realistic option. When coupled with grant money, since I was a single 21-year-old African American female taking care of myself, I could survive financially. Relieved, I only needed admission confirmation, and either school worked for me. While I was tremendously biased towards one university, God knew I would be happy anywhere. The promise had to be kept, period. Of course, the acceptance letter to the major research institution came a week later. The world belonged to me for just a moment.

Well, the semester drew to a close, and for whatever reason, I opted not to participate in Commencement, a decision I still regret. My village took great care of me and threw two college-bound parties, and I had almost everything I needed for the dorm. My promise was kept, and I moved into the dorm during the last week of August for First Flight Week, the week before classes began. First Flight week was perfect because my godmother dropped me off before she started school. I attended activities, got familiar with the campus, met my roommate, and interviewed with the director of the research program. The campus was big but beautiful, students were eclectic, and it was a dream come true.

What I did not know about the campus was the underlying climate for students of color. During “First Flight” week, I met several student organization leaders, including the President of the NAACP. He was walking around campus, spreading the need for change. While students of color were progressing at the university, the numbers were basically in a holding pattern. Student leaders hosted meetings with campus administration asking for more faculty of color, and a group of concerned students researched other institutions to identify plausible strategies to create a more inclusive climate. Rumors concerning minority quotas flowed freely. Faculty of color numbers were recruited in small numbers; however, faculty of color were exiting the university at a greater percentage. The NAACP and other primarily African American organizations formed a coalition and set to change the course for those coming behind them. Even more so, it seemed normal to see the university’s name or students on the news to address the climate changes that needed to take place. Unfortunately, I was naïve; I thought I would never be one of those students.

The next step was a mid-afternoon interview that I would never forget. I was dressed in business attire: Black slacks with thick wine stripes, a silk wine colored long sleeve blouse with a tie collar, popped by three-inch black soft leather heels and adorned with silver accessories. Obviously, the director liked me since they chose my essay, and I looked the part, so my mind was geared up. I grabbed my portfolio, made sure my ink pen worked, and headed to the meeting. As I entered the building, the atmosphere changed. The rooms were dark, but I could see pockets of light. The staff used lamps. Plants surrounded the room, but there was a not-so-friendly student that begrudgingly greeted me and asked me to take a seat. She said that the director would be with me shortly. I tried to keep smiling, but the fear that something was wrong gripped me. I twisted and turned, patted my feet, and tried to remember to breathe until the director showed up about twenty minutes later.

Finally, this short, thin, Caucasian, Texas-style redhead approaches me and introduces herself as director. We slowly walked to her lamp-lit office and sat; she pulled out my essay and began to ask me questions. All of a sudden, things seemed normal again. First, we had small talk, and I began to tell her somethings about me that would not be in the essay. Well, that was easy. Then it happened. She asked me for my name again. I politely responded with my full government name thinking that maybe I left out my middle name the first time. Next, she began to drill me about my essay. It would have been harmless, but the tone and macroaggressions, as well as passive-aggressiveness, made me feel extremely uncomfortable. Why was she asking me all these questions? Five questions dealt with my name, and if I was whom I claimed. Before this dreadful interrogation ended, she dissected my essay and said she wanted to assure I wrote it. Belittled beyond degree, her final questions forced me to relive the horrific accounts of my mother's murder again. I was confused, what was really happening. Finally, the meeting concluded with her saying that she was sorry, and the program did not have any money. What just happened to me? I needed the scholarship. Saddened and baffled, I quickly left my confidence and excitement in her office.

With tears streaming down my face, I rushed to my dorm room. All alone, I called my godmother, and immediately in her protective voice, she asked what I was going to do and if she needed to come and pick me up. I told her I needed to think about it. She had no idea that I was scrambling; my promise was about to be broken by one mean, hateful woman. I began to think of my network and remembered that I met the university's Dean of Students at the Leaders of Tomorrow Conference. I dug through my backpack and found his card. Maybe there was hope. First, I spoke with him over the phone. He did not remember me, but he did the conference and the African Student Organization. After assuring me he would look into the matter, he scheduled a meeting. When I arrived, to my surprise, the director of the program was invited as well. During the meeting, the dean repeatedly told me that I misunderstood. So now, frustration and anger enter the picture, because not only was I discriminated against based on my color, now I am being mistreated because of my youth. My gut was screaming for help, but I could not let the fear return. I managed to keep the fear down. The brief conversation concluded with the director telling me that she did not mean the program was out of funding, but that there was no remaining funding; I would be awarded after attaining a research position. They smiled as though the problem was solved; however, that feeling that I had as I waited for the interview--- returned. With no idea of how I could remain at the university without the stipend, I thanked them for the opportunity and declined admittance in the program altogether.

In conclusion, my first week at the university presented my first brush with racism and age discrimination. Yet, from those experiences, I learned my true strength and persevered. Declining the program forced me to take government loans to complete my degree as well as added years to pursuit. However, I did not let negative experiences hold me down. I joined several student organizations, became employed in student affairs, and worked diligently to assure that students on my watch would have an advocate. I did it… I kept my promise and graduated with a degree in English and returned to earn a master's degree in Higher Education. More so, I was privileged to serve as an advisory board member for the research program for over a decade and was the first staff member to receive an award that was given to faculty mentors.

My final analysis of racism and prejudice that we face in America is that we take our experiences, speak out, and work to ensure that things are better because we walked that path. Personally, I choose to work with civil rights organizations and volunteer to eradicate the –isms we face in our community. I believe that together, unified with one mission, we can make a difference.

About Cheylon

Cheylon Brown worked in cultural diversity and inclusion for over 22 years, serves as an educational consultant, co-founder of Crazy Faith Productions, founder of Cheylon Brown Ministries, and currently works in leisure services. Ms. Brown has a Bachelor of Arts degree in English, a master's degree in Higher Education, and certifications in Volunteer Community Resource Management, Supervisory Skills, and Managerial Skills. She is a Qualified Mediator and

Certified Etiquette Instructor. Most of all, she is a Christian that loves people.

Moreover, she is a motivational speaker. As a writer and poet, she had the opportunity to work with some wonderful people. She maintains strong ties with the community through service on advisory boards. Also, she is a Diamond Life member of Delta Sigma Theta Sorority, Inc. and a member of the NAACP. Because of her service to students and the community, Ms. Brown has received numerous awards and honors including the Diamonds and Pearls Community Image Award, as well as a Proclamation declaring May 30, 2015, as Cheylon Brown Day by the Mayor of Denton.

Finally, Cheylon Brown is a licensed evangelist, and in 2016, was ordained as an elder. She is the mother of two brilliant sons: DeMichael and Chason, and caretaker of her niece, Chevelle. She believes that "*If she stands tall, it is because she stands on the backs of those who came before her" (African Proverb).*

Chapter 5
"In the Key of Me"

By Janice Beecham

As people of color, we have endured things that we have had to smile through. My entire life, from a child to an adult, has been colored with racist experiences. The good thing is, I have been able to respond to racism in unusual ways where other people would say, "That couldn't have been me." What I knew to be true was, if I had retaliated with anger and hatred, I would have been reacting exactly the way they (the white racists I encountered) expected me to. Well, I'm better than that. Michelle Obama put it this way, "When they go low, we go high." Let's just say; I chose to soar because I have class. There are several experiences I could share with you, but for the sake of time, here are just a few.

My Son's Shoes

I received a call from my youngest son's principal about him stealing a pair of Nike shoes. He had never gotten into any trouble at school, and he knew better than to steal anything. I was not sure what this was all about. My son was wearing a pair of Nikes when he left for school that morning, so there was no need for him to take someone else's shoes. I had a feeling that the pair of Nikes the principal called me about belonged to my son, so I headed to the school to get his shoes back. After I got there and looked down at my child's feet, I noticed he was literally barefooted. He explained how the little white boy had taken his shoes from him. Sure enough, this little boy was wearing my son's shoes as if they were his! The principal refused to believe that my son could own an expensive pair of Nike shoes. I proceeded to share with him how I worked on a job and earned a living just like he did, and how I lived in a home that was probably nicer than his at the time. I could afford to buy my son an expensive pair of shoes if I wanted to, just like he could.

What the other little boy was boldly wearing on his feet were the shoes I paid for and the same shoes that had my son's name written on the inside with a permanent marker. Labeling my children's belongings was something I normally did, and on this day, it paid off. I told the principal that my son's name was written on the inside, and if he would simply take a minute to look, he would see for himself. After making the other little boy take the shoes off and glancing on the inside, he saw I was right. Just like I had mentioned, my son's name was clearly visible. It was only then that his shoes were returned.

"Now, you did all that! Don't you feel stupid?" I asked the principal, sarcastically. There was no response, no questions for the little boy regarding why he took my son's shoes, and no apology to either one of us. If only they would have investigated more, they would have identified who the real thief was before they even called me. Sadly, it was somehow easier to believe the lies of the little white boy over the truth of my black son.

No Restroom

My husband and I took a road trip to South Dakota. We have always enjoyed traveling together while delighting in each other's company. We decided to stop in a little town to get gas, plus I needed to use the restroom. There was a small gas station just up ahead, so we pulled in. I quickly hopped out of the car and went inside to use the ladies' room while my husband was preparing to get out and pay for gas. When I asked the clerk to use their restroom, he told me they did not have one. Disappointed, I strolled back to the car, where I waited patiently for my husband to finish pumping the gas. When he got back inside the car and started to buckle his seat belt, I told him what the clerk said. With a puzzled look on his face, he began to tell me how he had seen a white lady coming out of the restroom while he was inside paying for gas. So, the truth of the matter was, this was not a place that welcomed blacks, and I still had to pay my water bill, as some older people would say. Since I was not allowed to use the restroom inside of the store, we had to improvise because Mother Nature was surely not waiting for the next gas station. We had to do what we had to do. We drove away and found a spot on the side of the road that looked safe enough for us to stop. Yes, you guessed it right. I had to use the restroom on the side of the road, like some sort of animal. All because the racist clerk at the gas station did not want a black person using their restroom.

My Assignment

Trash duty! That is what they assigned me to, of all things. There were several men they could have put on trash duty, but they chose me, the only black employee in the group. This showed me how they felt about me. At first, I was very angry, and my attitude was not good. There were some not so nice things I wanted to say, but the Holy Spirit said, "Hold your peace!". So, I decided to smile and do my job with dignity. Although I knew this was meant to demean me, I still found a way to make it enjoyable. Some people were wondering how I could be so joyous on trash duty. What they didn't understand was, as a Christian woman, I believed I should give my best (my 100%) in whatever position I was in.

This was a situation designed to humiliate me, but what was meant for bad worked for my good. In the end, I wound up gaining favor with the boss. God used trash duty to make a connection that would benefit me in the long run.

Ice Cream Cone

It was the Wednesday before Thanksgiving, and I volunteered to work the ticket counter on this particular day. There was a flight delayed, and one of the customers, who happened to be a white man, was not happy about it. He continued to state how he needed to get to where he was going on time. My co-worker and I both explained that we had no control over the delayed flights, but that didn't change anything. He was still upset as he walked away and left the area for a while. He later returned, and his brewing anger was obvious. He approached me at the counter and asked, "Is the plane here?" I answered "No" and was completely caught off guard by what happened next. Out of the clear blue, he took his ice cream cone and smashed it directly in my face... right there in front of everybody. All you could hear were people gasping in shock and disbelief. Some wanted to know if I was okay. Honestly, I wanted to tear that man's head off, but I chose to respond differently by saying in a joking manner, "It's okay---but he should have at least gotten the right flavor." My response lightened the mood a bit, but I really could not believe he had just done that to me. My white co-worker was standing right beside me. Why me? Why did he smash his ice cream cone in my face? I honestly believe it was because my chocolate brown skin was not the right flavor!

Black Guy

My sister was in her twenties, but she still didn't know she was experiencing racism. She had a white friend/co-worker who liked to date black boys. My sister was having a conversation with her friend one day when she decided to ask her a question. She wanted to know if she would ever take any of the black guys that she dated home to meet her parents. After being asked the question, her friend was quick to respond by saying, "Oh no! I would NEVER do that!" My sister didn't understand how that could be the case. After all, she was a black girl and was allowed in their home. Surely, my sister wasn't the only black friend she was allowed to have. But why would her friend feel so uncomfortable inviting her black guy friend into their home? That is when she dropped the bomb. She admitted that her parents didn't like blacks. All that time, my sister was visiting the home of people who were considered to be her enemies. Wow! Wasn't that a slap in the face!

At Work

As a bookkeeper, customers would bring their checkbooks to the bank to be balanced. An older white lady came into the bank while my co-worker was at lunch. I had been asked to work at the front desk until she returned. The older lady dropped her checkbooks off at the front desk and made it known that she did not want me to balance hers. She wanted my co-worker to balance them, who was also a white woman.

Because I had been working long enough to observe and pick up on certain things, I noticed that the type of account the lady had, was costing her more money than the other type. I asked her why she had that type of account and told her that the other type would save her money. She did not believe me and told me I didn't know what I was talking about. I said to her, "Yes, I do." She still didn't believe me, so she asked the manager who confirmed, "Actually she's right. You would save money with the other account." Now the woman was wondering why she was never told she could save money with the other account. My co-worker came back from lunch, and the lady said to her, "That colored woman told me if I had this type of account, I could save money. "Her name is Janice." stated my co-worker. After the customer kept referring to me as "That colored woman," my co-worker became offended and repeated herself, this time in a firmer tone, "Her name is Janice!" The lady did not directly respond to her comment, but still wanted to know how it was that I knew about this type of account, but my co-worker did not seem to have knowledge. It blew her mind that I knew something my co-worker did not know.

The next time the woman came into the bank, I spoke to her, and these were her words: "When we give you niggers an inch, you want a mile." I sarcastically replied by saying, "No...I want five." This wasn't my only prejudice encounter while working at the bank. There were times when white customers would enter the building and refuse to take a seat if I offered the empty chair. It was apparent they would rather stand than sit in a chair offered by a black person. I often wondered while working for the bank, how was it that I was good enough to train people on the job, but I was never good enough for the job. So, I asked my boss, and he blatantly admitted, "It's because you're black."

Growing Up

Growing up as a black child, I experienced a lot of racism. My grandfather lived on a decent-sized farm. He would often take me to the store with him, but the white owner never allowed me to come inside. He would tell my grandfather I had to stay outside until he finished with his business. There were also times I would go with my father to his job. He parked cars for a living, and the white guy at the parking lot would ask him, "Who's that gal you got with you?" Daddy would answer, "That's my daughter. She's not a gal."

Then there was integration. I am reminded of how the white students treated us, black kids. They were rude and mean towards us. I vividly recall how we were not allowed to swim in the pool with the white kids. All because they felt like we were dirty. I guess my brother could no longer fight off temptation because one day, he got into the pool to swim. No sooner than he had gotten his body wet, I watched as a white lady came and made all the white kids get out. Even though this was extremely embarrassing, the good thing was, my brother, did have the whole swimming pool to himself. It just depends on how you look at it. But that wouldn't last long because they would drain the water from the swimming pool after any black people entered the water, for fear that it was contaminated.

In middle school, I wanted to be a cheerleader. The black girls could try out for the cheer squad, but they had absolutely no intention of picking any of us, so I'm not sure why they wasted our time. In high school, there was both a black cheer squad and a white cheer squad that was known to be racist. The white cheerleaders would do things to try and get the black cheerleaders kicked off the campus.

I can also remember in "" Homemaking" class how we would have to cook different meals. The teachers and the white students never wanted to taste the food that the black students prepared. One day, however, the teacher messed around and tasted our food. Our menu included chicken, mashed potatoes, green beans, and cornbread on that day. As much as she wanted to, she could not stop eating. Suddenly, it went from her not wanting to taste our food to her asking us how we prepared it and what ingredients we used. Ain't that something!

Still Alive

Racism is still alive and well. My most recent experiences have happened as an adult. On one occasion, my family was enjoying a day at the fair. It was at the food court that an older white couple was already seated. After we sat down beside them, the couple wrapped their food up and moved to another table, just to keep from sitting near us.

On a separate occasion, I had an encounter in a public restroom with an older white woman. She and another lady were waiting to use the restroom. After I came out of the stall, I heard her say to the other lady, “That colored lady just came out of there, I’m not going in there.” I had to let her know right then and there that I was not the nasty one. Believe it or not, this is something that just happened recently, within the last two years. Proof that racism is still very much alive today.

Barbecue Man

My experience with racism that sticks out the most, however, is the one with the barbecue man. My good girlfriend and I ate at a barbecue restaurant several years ago, and I noticed the ketchup tasted kinda weird. I shared my concern with the owner of the restaurant, and what he did, I will NEVER forget. He snatched up the butcher knife from the cutting block, looked me straight in the eyes, and in a mean voice, told me he would stick that knife inside of me and twist my guts. I was in total shock and disbelief! Then I became furious. I was so angry! Can you believe that? My life was threatened, and I was utterly humiliated in a restaurant full of people, all because I told this man the ketchup tasted weird. My friend wanted us to leave, but my pride would not let me walk out. She kept saying, "Let's go!" and I replied with confidence, "I'm not going!" When she and I finally left the restaurant, two white men followed us out. They started apologizing to me for what happened. What I couldn't understand was why they never spoke up when the incident occurred. They had the opportunity to defend me and speak up for what was right if they felt I wasn't being treated fairly. But, they chose to remain silent.

Fast forward. Years later, after that incident, I walked into an establishment and was shocked to see who the kitchen cook was. Of all people, it was the barbecue man. The same one who had threatened my life years ago. The ugly memories of those evil things he said to me came seeping to the forefront of my mind, triggering my emotions. I told the server how he had threatened me with a knife years ago, and I made sure I said it loud enough for him to hear me. I could see his face turning beet red, but he didn't say anything. There was no acknowledgment of what he had done, and no apology was offered. I let the server know, "As long as that man works here, I'm not spending my money here.", and then I left. This? This is the incident that has stuck with me for years, even up until this very day. I did not deserve to be treated that way!

Now that I have painted a visual, it is apparent how the evil acts of racism have been sprinkled throughout my life. As a wife, mother, and grandmother who has lived through and survived this type of treatment, my prayer is that people who don't necessarily look like us would see us through God's eyes because he created us all equal. Our world is driven by ignorance. I realize that sometimes people react because of what they don't know, but God doesn't see color. He sees us as His creation. I pray that God eradicates racism on this earth. I pray that He proves himself and who He is to this nation, and that He touches the hearts of people. I pray that we can love the way God loves. Love has no color!

I Corinthians 13: 4-8a "Love suffers long and is kind; love does not envy; love does not parade itself, is not puffed up; does not behave rudely, does not seek its own, is not provoked, thinks no evil; does not rejoice in iniquity, but rejoices in the truth; bears all things, believes all things, hopes all things, endures all things. Love never fails."

About Janice

First Lady Janice Beecham describes herself as a country girl from Ennis, Texas, who currently resides in the city of DeSoto. Worshipper, mentor, and vessel of grace are the characteristics of this anointed and powerful woman of God. She married her high school sweetheart, Pastor R.C. Beecham III, and 46 years later, their love still kindles. They are blessed to have three wonderful sons, Rodney (Wendy), Marcus (Shaun), Brandon (Dajia), and six beautiful grandchildren, Cameron, Landon, Hailey, London, Loryn, and R.C. Beecham IV.

Lady Beecham is the First Lady of the Greater New Vision Christian Center, where she has served faithfully providing leadership, love, and loyal support for 34 years alongside her husband, Pastor R.C. Beecham III. Lady Beecham worked ten years for Southwest Airlines before leaving the corporate world to serve full time in the ministry with her husband. They have been blessed to travel the world, evangelizing, and sharing their compelling and life-changing testimonies.

Lady Beecham serves as the President of the Women's Department. As a result of Lady Beecham's passion for seeing women live at their fullest God-given potential, she organized a women's ministry called "Inside Out Women's Ministry." Through this ministry, a premier mentoring program for young ladies was birthed to teach young girls their value and worth. It was affectionately named "Always a Lady."

First Lady Beecham has truly dedicated her life to serving God and his people. Indeed, a warrior for the Kingdom, she has demonstrated extreme faith while overcoming the woes of breast cancer, chemotherapy, and Covid-19. She is a woman of grace and strength and a firm believer in God and his Word. First Lady Beecham is often heard quoting her favorite scripture, "*...those who know their God shall be strong and do exploits.*" (Daniel 11:32b)

Chapter 6
"The Unfairness of Discrimination"

By Sylvia D. Chandler Shaw

The personal encounters that I experienced within a Black family growing up in the South made me angry. The problems I encountered were a lack of neighborhood resources, school segregation, and the unfair housing practices by individuals who did not want to accept and abide by the law. These experiences became a way of life for many of our families. We persevered through these issues, in hopes that one day we would see positive changes that would make things better.

The Lack of Neighborhood Resources

Growing up in the early '60s was a difficult time for my family. We moved from Orange Mound, which is considered the inner city, to country living. This move took place in hopes of establishing a family dwelling in another part of town known as the Acklena Community. My parents were in search of a better life for themselves. I was the youngest of the siblings when they moved. When my parents moved to the neighborhood, there were no houses. The community, as a whole, had not been developed. The street that I grew up on was George Road. Some of the neighboring streets were Hewlett Road, Delta Road, Ford Road, Honduras Road, Eighth Road, and Southaven. The school I attended was our neighborhood school, Geeter High School.

Growing up, we had no indoor toilets or running water. We used outer houses for bathrooms, and my parents pumped our water from a well on the property. As neighbors, we had to share resources to survive. There was an article written by Aubrey Ford, Phoebe Weinman & Walker Weinman titled, "Boxtown: The Land of Broken Promises." This article details the lack of resources that plagued the Boxtown community. Boxtown was a neighboring community in which we share a similar story. Requests were made to the city by my father and other neighbors within the community. The requests were to help improve our standards of living by adding plumbing, water lines, and sewers in our neighborhood.

Many years passed before anything was done to help our community. Why did it take so long? We were tax-paying citizens too! I felt that we were experiencing discrimination by way of services. Areas in Whitehaven did not experience the lack of services as we did. Simply put, we were black citizens in that part of the County. During that time, funds were not allocated to improve the living conditions for us as Shelby County Citizens.

A major overhaul took place on January 1, 1970 (Annexation). We were annexed into the City of Memphis, which we thought would resolve painful issues that we had faced for so many years. Little did we know our situation worsened. Some parts of the neighborhood received some services, but some did not. The annexation benefitted white communities. We noticed over time how white communities began to expand tremendously. How did this happen? How were newer communities being established so quickly? Here we were, with yet still a dilemma! Although we were citizens of Memphis, we continued to have limited resources. The families in our community remained hopeful. Our parents never gave up. Improvements to the neighborhood eventually took place, but in certain areas.

School Segregation

After graduating from my neighborhood school (Geeter High School) in 1972, like many of my neighborhood friends, we started a new chapter in life. We started pursuing education and career jobs. Employment opportunities increased, which allowed many African Americans the ability to qualify for jobs as a result of the Civil Rights Act of 1964.

Many of my friends and family who were underclassmen were not as fortunate as we were to remain in the Neighborhood School. Busing soon took place. Our neighborhoods were torn apart. Families were being forced to adhere to the school bus laws which caused the separation of families and friends to schools that were miles apart from their homes. Parents were being advised that this would provide better educational opportunities for their children. My younger siblings told our parents many times about the treatment they were given because of the color of their skin. They felt unwelcome, unwanted, and disrespected. My siblings were experiencing racial discrimination.

Certainly, a difference was being made in their treatment. Although the lunch was the same for everyone, it was still segregated, not to mention other school activities as well. White flight had taken place and many of the students that once lived in the community moved. The decision was made by their parents to get out of Whitehaven. These actions were a result of school integration.

Things have changed over time. My best friend Sharon and my sister Elizabeth attended the first-ever class reunion, where both parties in the alumni enjoyed each other's company. This reunion provided a welcomed, wanted, and respected celebration. There was more of a cohesiveness. As the years passed, the hearts of many of the alumni changed with a desire to promote healing and make things better.

Housing

In 1976 I married Raymond Earl Shaw Sr., who had just returned from his tour in South Korea. Right before the wedding, we began our search for our first apartment. We were so excited, finally starting our new life together. We began our search for locations that we could afford. Needless to say, the locations we chose in our budget were not in a desirable part of town. We were hoping to find an apartment near our jobs. The apartments that we contacted had "apartments for rent" signs posted on their premises. We set out to start applying. The apartment complexes that we contacted sounded favorable. The tones in our voices disclosed that we were African Americans. Once they figured out by our voice that we were African Americans, what was once a vacancy, was now all of a sudden filled. Everywhere we inquired, it was the same results. No vacancies. We decided to stop calling the offices and use a different approach. We started showing up on the spot and asking if we could apply for an apartment. My husband and I still were not successful in our search. At this point, we felt defeated. Here we were looking forward to starting our new life together in a place of our own. We were devastated! I had a gut feeling that we were being discriminated against because of our race.

Why would these leasing managers still not want to adhere to the law? Why would these individuals try to prevent us from fulfilling our dreams? We were hurt, but we did not let that end our quest in search of an apartment. In other words, we were not going to give up. We would continue to look for decent housing until we found the right one.

I shared my experience with a couple of my co-workers, who said this could not be happening. One day, they noticed how quiet I was and asked what was bothering me. I was apprehensive about discussing my problems at work, but I was relieved once I shared with them what was happening. My co-workers knew that we had started our apartment search, and even they had given us suggestions on locations to apply. The very thought of this still happening made them share in my pain. After all the discrimination laws that were passed to help African Americans, why would we still be faced with being discriminated against?

One of my coworkers, who happened to be Caucasian, said, "I bet you have been getting denied because you sound black." She stated, "You should call this apartment complex and ask if they have vacancies. See what they tell you. If they say no, hang-up, and I will call back". Sure enough, I was told there were no vacancies. My co-worker called back a few minutes later. She asked if they had any vacancies. The manager asked her what she was interested in. She stated, "A one-bedroom or a two-bedroom." The leasing manager replied, “Yes, we have vacancies for both.” I was shocked and outraged at what this experiment exposed. Although I was hurt and angry, I decided that I did not want to go through all the hassle of reporting the incident. I felt that it would not be worth the worry and stress to pursue the matter further. Some things in life, you have to learn how to let go. I feel like I made the right decision. I decided to pray about it and not worry.

We did eventually find an apartment that we were approved for. They had vacancies because a large percentage of the whites were moving out once they learned that African Americans could potentially be moving into their neighborhoods. We lived in the apartment for two years, before deciding that we wanted to purchase a home. As I stated earlier, my husband was a Veteran, so the process was a much better experience. We were able to use his Veteran's benefits to qualify for a home.

In place of all the negative experiences that I encountered from discriminatory acts, there was a light at the end of the tunnel. To this day, I remain hopeful that we can learn how to love and respect all people regardless of race and rid our society of racial discrimination. After all, we are all trying to live our best life. Let us do it together!

About Sylvia

Sylvia D. Chandler-Shaw is a native Memphian. She is a proud mother, grandmother, and great grandmother. As a Songstress, she is most passionate about working with the music ministry at her church.

Sylvia is newly retired from the City of Memphis as an Operations Analyst. She received her Master of Science Degree in Operations Management.

In her spare time, she enjoys reading, watching movies, and spending quality time with her family.

Chapter 7
"Mirrored Reflections"

By Audrey Guyden Allen

Proverbs 22:6 says, *"Train up a child in the way he should go, and when he is old he will not depart from it."* I have realized as I've grown that God has a unique plan for each of our lives. My mother raised me to rely and depend on God for everything. Through her teaching and training, I realized that the things she taught me would be the very things I needed to succeed in life. As I've gotten older, I've come to the conclusion that situations don't always determine the outcome of your life, and God has made each of us unique and gifted. As I reflect on my pilgrimage and the things my mother taught me, I can't help but consider all she must have endured. She was an amazing woman, and I knew that one day I would have my own experiences that would shape the woman I would become.

Janie D. Rodgers was born in 1914 to Mary and Will Rogers in Arcadia, Louisiana. Mary and Will raised a total of 7 children. They grew up and picked cotton on a land that was passed down from his grandfather, Barry Rogers. Barry Rogers was a white judge in Arcadia, Louisiana. Though Grandpa Barry lived close by, twice a year, the Ku Klux Klan would torment the Rogers Family by burning crosses in the field near their home. Will Rogers confronted them with his voice raised, "Never come back again!"

My mother was reared in a Christian household under the tutelage of her father and grandfather. She learned Christian values and developed an early love for oration and teaching. At the age of 12, she was asked to teach Sunday school. At the age of 14, she was offered an opportunity to teach in Africa as a missionary. However, the offer would go unaccepted due to her mother's unexpected death. It was at that moment; my mother began raising her younger siblings. Her older siblings were married and pursuing their careers. After her baby sister Mary Etta married, she moved to Ft. Worth, Texas in 1936, with only $8 in her pocket. After being in Fort Worth only two days, she secured a job at a steakhouse near downtown Ft. Worth and was hired as a cook.

In the midst of racial discourse, Janie suffered discrimination daily. Her first encounter was with her jealous white coworker, who was intimidated by her cooking. All the while, she didn't know Janie was the best cook back home, one of the best cooks in all of Louisiana. The white woman began to mock her and call her names. Janie didn't want to retaliate, so she decided to quit. To her surprise, the co-worker was fired, and Janie was rehired. God was ordering her footsteps every step of the way, and she began to carve out a new life for herself in Texas.

She often told her children that her prayer was, "Lord, guide me and protect me, order my footsteps, and I will serve you till the day I die." The prayer of protection was common amongst blacks, for they surely had to depend on God to protect them from the violent acts of racism.

Six months later, she met and married Frazier Guyden. Respectively, to their union, three children were born: Gwendolyn, Kenneth, and Audrey Guyden. The family joined the city's first Black Baptist church, now known as the Historical Greater St. James Baptist Church, under the leadership of Rev. C.A. Holiday. Being founded back in the 1800s, I'm sure this church experienced its fair share of racial injustices. As a devoted Christian to the faith and her church, my mother was asked to speak at the Black Baptist Convention regularly, as she was a wonderful orator. Her oration of the poem "Beware of Church Dudes" frequently made her the highlight of various church and community functions. Many nights, she would travel to and from the conventions, having to stop in towns that seemed proud to be racists. They awaited opportunities to harass and mistreat black people as they traveled through, heading to their destinations.

Never a woman to mince words, my mother said what she meant and meant what she said. Although some may have found her words stern, it was always said in love. With that same love, she would explain the importance of family and friends, and to "love one another" as the Bible commands. She made it a point to remind family and friends of Joel 1:3, "Tell it to your children and let your children tell their children, and their children to the next generation." Her goal was to ensure that family and friends understood the importance of their family history, as a reminder of how far

God had brought them. Although her father's father was a white man, she had been raised in Louisiana, where racism was wide and prevalent. As a result, she frequently reminded family and friends of how God always protects and provides, and how important it is to appreciate his grace and mercy daily. It was also equally important to her that her family understood, respected, and valued their own history. A history filled with racism, but also great courage and spirit.

Her confidence in herself exuded through the command of her voice and her very presence. She emphasized that the color of my skin didn't determine my value. She often reminded me that our ancestors were slaves, and their names were changed, stripping them of their true identity. It was important to her that I didn't have a negative attitude about my dark melanin skin. Every day she would make me look at myself in the mirror, and she would say, "Look at yourself. Do you look good to you?" If you think you look good, then everyone thinks you look good." She wanted to instill in me that if I didn't know who I was, people would define me. It was important that I defined myself. She wanted me to understand that no one had the right to steal my identity and define me to fit their idea of what they thought I should be. She wanted me to know my value.

Much like my mother, I would experience some of the same racial disparities she experienced. My skin tone, hair texture, knowledge, and skills would often be scrutinized by others. I began a career in the banking industry in 1978 as a bookkeeper. During my tenure, I experienced continuous discrimination. I was accused of stealing $20. Not $50---not $100. And as the only Black employee, I was forced to take a lie detector test. I failed the test. I explained to my supervisor that I was not guilty. After repeatedly explaining that I had not taken the money, the polygraph examiner stated that if I was on my menstrual cycle during the exam, it could result in failing the test. I felt so disrespected and bullied because of my skin color. They told me I could retake the test the following month. During my wait, I was under a lot of pressure. I was going through separation and facing divorce, I had surgery, coworkers were gossiping about me, and they even had me under surveillance at work. Within the next month, I was able to retake the test. This time I passed. Despite the racism, I remained at the bank for years, witnessed five corporate transitions, and my dedication to the work I was doing warranted three promotions.

I eventually worked my way to a supervisor's position, working the weekend schedule. There would soon be another incident where I would be accused of stealing. Two-thousand dollars went missing, and I was soon under investigation by the FBI. I was the only Black female working at the same bank for years and was being accused of being a thief. I served and dedicated all my time to this company, "How could they do this to me?", I thought. After weeks of investigation, it was concluded that I had nothing to do with the incident, and without cause, I was demoted. I never received an apology or any vindication from anyone at the bank. There was also no admission that they had accused the wrong person. I continued to work for the bank, but now I was filled with anxiety, frustration, and rage. I chose to remain dedicated to my work because I needed the job to provide for my girls.

As a result of my experiences, I now realize that when problems interrupt our lives, they are not always meant for destruction. God's divine plan for our lives has a divine purpose. God uses both the good and bad, the positive and the negative, for our ultimate good. We have the ability to turn our negatives into positives, but the journey may not be easy. The trials of racial injustice have delayed my journey, but in those trials, the Holy Spirit of God would confirm that he was always with me. I heard the Holy Spirit say, “Who has carried you this far? Haven't I, your God, supplied all your needs? When have you ever not had any money? Have you ever gone hungry? Have you ever gone without clothing? What makes you think I would leave you now?”

All of the lessons my mother taught me prepared me to live and navigate in a world that may not appreciate my worth. I have learned not to resist situations. If I run from them, they run after me. God’s divine intervention (my experiences) has set me up for my blessings.

I have learned to define myself, as my mother taught me. No matter the skin tone, caramel or ebony, light or dark-skinned---I matter. My mother instilled in me a sense of self-worth, self-care, and self-love, as God loves me. Psalms 57:2 states, “I cry out to God Most High, to God who fulfills his purpose in me.” I have learned to call out to God and listen to the Holy Spirit to ensure I understand God’s purpose for my life.

About Audrey

Audrey Jane Guyden-Allen was born on January 28th to the union of Frazier and Janie Guyden. A very dear friend of hers, Jewel Kelly, once told her, "You never tell your age." Audrey is not ashamed of her birth date--in fact, she is actually grateful, but she has followed her friend's golden advice, keeping her year of birth suspenseful. Audrey believes age puts a limit on one's ability, and she is determined that age will not define her capacity.

Audrey was the third child and the Baby Girl of her family. She was born to a United States Army soldier and a mother of many skills. In her mother's house, the rule was "Do what you are told and do not question it" therefore, attending church was a must and not an option in her mother and father's home.

From kindergarten to first grade, Audrey attended "I Mother Mercy," a Catholic school for African American children. She later enrolled in Versia L. Williams. Versia was her choir director at St. James Baptist Church, where she acquired a love and passion for music and dance under her tutelage. According to Audrey, some of the best of times were, spending long summer evenings listening to the infamous Grambling Tiger Marching Band and enjoying the culture of Grambling, Louisiana, with her cousin.

Audrey started high school in 1969 and graduated in 1974. Her class was the first class to be integrated at Amon Carter Riverside High School in Ft. Worth, Texas. After graduation, she attended Flight Airline Training for Delta Airlines in Kansas, Missouri. She would later return to Ft. Worth, Texas to marry William Allen, have her firstborn child, and eleven years later, her second child.

Audrey worked in the banking industry for 33 years and was blessed to be a top salesman throughout the years. In 2003, she attended Texas Institute Massage and then retired from Wells Fargo in 2008. After retiring, she started her own business "Rapha Massage." She has been a traveling massage therapist for 15 years.

Audrey states, "My greatest accomplishments are my two children, Tamara Allen and Sharde' Allen." Audrey can't wait to see what God is going to do next in her life. She strongly believes He is not through with her yet.

Chapter 8
"Brown Girls in IT"

By Demira Devoil

Life can be surreal at times. I recall standing in the middle of a village in Egypt as a missionary, thinking, "How did a little Black girl from a small town in Louisiana get here?" As a Black woman in a STEM (Science, Technology, Engineering, and Mathematics) career, there have been several times in my life that I have had these surreal moments and feelings while working in corporate America. Growing up as a child in the '90s, the technology boom in the early 2000s sparked my interest in having a career in IT. Having a career in IT became all I could think about, and I put my all into having those dreams realized. I graduated from the best HBCU on the planet, Southern University A&M College. In college, I learned a lot about what was expected of me as a Black woman, an employee, and how to do my job, but it didn't prepare me for how the world would perceive or receive a Black woman as a Software Engineer.

While preparing for my first day as a Senior Software Engineer, I had no idea what to expect. My only contact at the time was the contracting company that hired me, so walking into a new company and a new work team, I was filled with joy but still nervous. I sat in the team meeting, looking around. I noticed that out of a team of about thirty people, I was the only Black woman, and there was one Black man mixed in with other races such as Indian, Vietnamese, and Caucasian. My new Black male coworker turned to me and said, "They didn't see you before you got here, huh?" I smiled and said, "No, I had all phone interviews." So, when I showed up for my first day, it was their first time meeting me. I learned later that his statement to me was to warn me that in his twenty years with the company, he had seen Black women come and go, but they did not stick around for long. It was on that day that I learned two big lessons as a Black woman while working in the IT field. The first lesson was always to negotiate your pay to what you believe your worth is, and don't be afraid to say, "I would like to be paid more." The racial injustice that occurred at this job was that I was being paid way lower than my other coworkers, who were less qualified. I had a bachelor's and a master's degree, coupled with about seven years of experience, which put me in the category of a Senior Software Engineer. I had the title--- but not the pay.

It wasn't until about three months later, after having a performance review, that I found out I was being paid about $30,000 less than other coworkers who didn't have the educational background, and nowhere near the amount of experience I encompassed. According to the Institute for Women's Policy Research (2019), "Black women are paid 38% less than white men and 21% less than white women". I must admit that I was a bit infuriated because I worked twice as hard as my work counterparts to make sure I was always on top of my game. Being the only Black woman in a corporate American environment brings about a pressure that other races cannot relate too. There is a feeling of having to be successful in all that you do, or else the other races will judge your race as a whole, based on your performance. I remember calling my recruiter and discussing my concerns with the pay disparity, and his response to me was, there was nothing he could do, and maybe next time, "I should negotiate better!". This was most definitely one of the surreal moments in my life where I could not believe I was in the shoes of other Black women that I'd heard these kinds of stories from and about. The only issue I had with his statement was, it was never relayed to me that the pay was negotiable and that the amount I agreed upon was the only amount that could be given. I stayed with the company for a couple of years after, but deep down inside, I always resented working there because I knew I was not being compensated for what I was worth, and I didn't feel valued.

We, as Black women, often have the tendency to stay in places and spaces where we are not growing or valued. Before this experience, I was made aware of gender and race disparities in pay by the stories of other Black women, but I had never had an encounter with it myself. I will admit, I became passive about the situation. Being a single mom at the time, I felt if I had pressed the issue, I would have lost my job. I wasn't in a position to be without income; therefore,

I stayed with less pay and no raise for about two years. This encounter taught me that people see me as what I see within myself. It opened my eyes up to what others believe my value is within their company, and no matter what I feel, that is what I am worth. If I don't fight for it, they will tell me my value. My greatest hope is that more young Black girls and women will seek out careers in STEM. I want them to know that it is okay to be an anomaly within the IT field. I want them to be unapologetically awesome in all that they do, so I share this story to encourage others to know your value and what you bring to the table, and never settle for less.

References

Institute for Women's Policy Research, "The Gender Wage Gap: 2018" (September 2019), https://iwpr.org/wp-content/uploads/2019/09/C484.pdf. LeanIn.Org calculates the 21% gap between Black and white based on IWPR data.

About Demira

Demira Devoil is a native of Bastrop, Louisiana, and currently resides in Fort Worth, Texas. Presently, she is the CEO and founder of Devoil Solutions LLC, an IT consulting company.

In 2017, Demira founded Hopeful Arms Foundation, which is a 501c (3) non-profit organization established to provide intensive life planning, financial planning training, education, and other services to high risk, underserved individuals. Their mission is to stop the cycle of poverty by saturating the single parent and homeless population with the tools and resources to succeed.

Demira also has the role of an author. In 2018, she authored a journal line, "Journals By Hopeful Arms," which is designed to encourage beautiful souls to be their best selves regardless of what stage of life they find themselves.

Recently, she became a Doctoral Candidate while in pursuit of a doctorate in Organizational Leadership at Grand Canyon University. She is the mother of a beautiful daughter, an active leader, a servant in the community, a philanthropist, and a modern-day missionary.

Chapter 9
"Powers Oppressing the Pupil"

By Terri Alford, M.Ed.

It was a Friday morning in the Spring of 2007, and I was excited as ever. I ironed my favorite white blouse with yellow polka dots and my black skirt the night before so that I could be at school bright and early for the National High School Honor Society induction. The ceremony was held in the library during the first period. I sat next to the only student present upon arrival. She had a familiar face, but for some reason, we did not exchange names. We chatted for a minute until a classmate came to the table where we were sitting. She addressed me by the first name when saying hello, and the girl asked, “What's your last name?” When I replied, “Alford,” astoundingly, she asked, “YOU are Terri Alford? I have heard a lot about you, but I thought you were White!” I became mute; no appropriate response was possible. I knew exactly what she meant. She had been competing with me academically and admitted to hearing teachers talk highly about me all the time.

I was in the top ten of our junior class of over 300 students. Instead of being proud, I felt as if I would never be good enough. Until that moment, I had never felt so uncomfortable in my own skin. As a self-conscious teen with low self-esteem and few true friends, I was excited at the possibility of becoming part of a social group in which I would be accepted and build life-long relationships. Instead,

I was reminded that I was too different to just "fit-in" anywhere. Now I dare to be different.

Over the years, I can recall countless times the color of my skin brought microaggressions and unwelcomed racist commentary, which led me to internalize racism. Microaggressions are the everyday slights, putdowns, indignities, and insults that a marginalized population uses to oppress a population of people. They appear to be a compliment but contain a hidden insult within them. Some are verbal, while others are nonverbal.

For example, I can recall going to a new beauty supply store owned by Asian Americans. I had time on my hand, so I browsed the store, taking inventory visually of what all they had so I could see if it was worth the drive to cross state lines and go to this new store for my hair needs. I was followed and watched so closely that I felt uncomfortable. Whenever I made direct eye contact with an employee, a nervous "Can I help you find something?" was their subtle attempt to justify following me. The way I was followed in the near-empty store and asked if I needed help multiple times was a nonverbal microaggression that African Americans are prone to. The crime- in this case, theft.

Too often, when people think of racist remarks made towards a Black person, they think the use of the word "Nigger" is involved. However, most of my experiences with racism has included microaggressions, actions, and gestures that were used to disempower me or remind me that my skin color should make me a second-class citizen in the country that is supposed to be my own.

Black.
I am black and black is me.
I pity myself for being so ugly.
From the top of my head to the bottom of my peeling feet
I see flaws within and upon me.

Short.
Short nappy hair and I'm short in stature.
Shortcomings and insecurities
Enabling bullies to exploit my look with laughter

What is beautiful that has come from darkness?
What dark being has been recognized for the beauty it possesses?
How can I believe otherwise when I've allowed the lies about my appearance to manifest?
I guess I will just work to be known as the smart girl and forget about the rest…

I just gave you a sneak peek into my elementary mindset. Yes, I worked hard because my parents instilled in me to always do my best, but I had a secret agenda. I wanted my identity to derive from what I knew, how I applied knowledge, and for the person, I was on the inside. As an adult, I still want to be perceived in such a way, but the difference between then and now is I accept, embrace, and love how I look and I am. My skin tone, short hair, shorter limbs, smaller feet, blemished face, small waist, wide hips, full lips, full calves, contagious laugh, bright smile, and engaging eyes are all components of me. These attributes make me who I am. I am no longer ashamed of my culture, my appearance, my race, or my identity.

I grew up on the border of Mississippi and Tennessee. I spent most of my childhood in Desoto county, which is known for being the "Top of Mississippi" in more ways than one.

I went to school in Memphis, Tennessee, from kindergarten to the second grade. My first elementary school was predominantly black and known for being low performing and dangerous. As a matter of fact, it is no longer standing. In the third grade, I moved from Memphis to Southaven, Mississippi- literally a five-minute drive. I've always loved school, learning, and experiencing new things, yet I didn't know the challenge I was up against. It was there I learned I was black for the first time. My third-grade class had three students that were black. I was the only black girl, and there were two black boys. I was noticeably different. My hair was different. My skin was different. I hit puberty early, so even my body looked different, and my classmates never let me forget it.

I remember thinking (and hoping) that one of the prettiest and most popular girls was heading my way on the playground to ask me to play with her and her friends. Instead, she accused me of stuffing my bra, when I didn't even know what that meant. I remember being referred to as having black skin and not brown because my skin was dark. A brown crayon wasn't the right color to use because it wasn't dark enough. I was called "chocolate" so much that I only drank white milk in school. Every time we heard the word "villain," the words dark, ugly, and black were used. Every movie or video clip with a villain in it always depicted the villain as evil, nothing positive about a dark character in the story. I couldn't help but wonder if that was the reason why no one wanted to play with me on the playground. I guess I looked like a villain.

I had friends at my old elementary school, but at this elementary school, I couldn't fit in. I began to internalize that my blackness was ugly. Therefore, I had made up in my mind as a small child that I wanted my children not to look like me. I wanted my children to have fair skin, light eyes, long curly hair, and no chances of having the feelings I had about having black skin.

In high school, I can remember taking advanced classes, and every year on the first day of school, I would always wonder how many black students were going to be in my class. By the time I was a high schooler the county was more diverse. Our student body was about 50% Caucasian and 50% minority. So, there were enough of "us" for the classrooms to be more diverse, but they were not. I remember white classmates referring to me as "one of the smart black" classmates. I remember arguing with a student in the 10th grade about working hard to earn scholarships while he proceeded to tell me that I had an unfair advantage because people will feel sorry for me being black. I recall when I got hired for my first job at the age of fifteen, one of the managers said that she thought I was white when they saw my application and letters of recommendation. She too was surprised such accolades belonged to a fifteen-year-old black girl.

I didn't stop at grade school. I experienced more of it in college and in the workplace. Specifically, I remember one professor that had no shame in the racist remarks that he made. As a matter of fact, he seemed to be proud of the fact that he was a racist and a sexist, and he dared people to debate him instead of teaching content for his business class.

Through many years of striving to overcome internalized racism and self-hate, I found my identity in falling in love with me. I experienced racism as an educator, school leader, financial services professional, and entrepreneur, but the difference is, what caused me to hate myself and feel unworthy only made me stronger and love my race more.

My Creator created a masterpiece in creating me, and I thank him for giving me the privilege to walk this Earth as a Black Queen. “I praise you, for I am fearfully and wonderfully made. Wonderful are your works; my soul knows it very well.” -Psalm 139:14 Many powers, systems of oppression, and principalities hindered me from experiencing joy and self-love as a pupil, but now I am empowered to fight racism while loving who I see in the mirror at the same time.

About Terri

Terri Alford is a former principal turned entrepreneur and economic empowerment educator.

Terri owns TNA Financial Management: Helping individuals, families, and businesses become debt-free, retire with dignity, get money when you need it most, secure your income, and build wealth. She educates families with proven strategies and financial principles to build generational wealth. She has been a licensed insurance agent since 2015, and her agency serves families in fifteen states. Her clientele is valued from the first appointment, and she continues to foster relationships throughout the years. She works diligently to ascertain what are her client needs and find solutions to meet the needs. Financial freedom is the goal!

Terri Alford serves as the economic empowerment chair for Dallas-Fort Worth Urban League of Young Professionals, in which she leads a committee creating a coalition of change agents that are passionate about narrowing the wealth gap in DFW. During 2020-2021, the committee will deliver programming, resources, and experiences that will help young professionals grow into the best versions of themselves from a financial and/or business perspective.

Terri Alford is also the owner and founder of Principles From The Principal, LLC ™, created to educate, empower, and equip single Christian women to Live Happily Ever NOW. She is a role model to many but a mother and wife to none (yet). She teaches women that singleness is a gift, so this season should be maximized! Thus, take advantage of the opportunities that are before you because they will not always be there. Not only is this a different mindset, but it is also a boss mindset that promotes other qualities and disciplines such as time management, networking, and service.

You can find Terri speaking in churches, in schools, at conferences, and any place there's a platform to serve others by sharing her knowledge.

Chapter 10
"My Pain. My Story. My Victory"

By Dr. Anita Allen Penn

I had plans and aspirations that I would have a great marriage and have children who would become important trend-setters and world changers. My wish was that they would resemble me and have mannerisms and physical traits that identified who they belong to. But what happens when those desires are overcome with the reality that your child has a genetic disorder and chronic illness? How do you balance love and fear in a healthy manner when faced with the fact that a diagnosed disorder of one child will affect the trajectory of the entire family unit?

Divorced. Depressed. Overweight. Unhealthy. Unemployed. Embarrassed. Afraid. Angry. How does one live a balanced lifestyle with these odds? Millions of questions swarmed around in my head, but I could not verbalize even one. Maybe I was just having an out of body experience—Ha, wishful thinking. How did "I" end up in this place? I'm an educated Black woman who comes from a rich legacy of family strength, dedication, and high morals and values. What did I do to earn this set of circumstances?

Unfortunately, I became comfortable with my losses. I cannot say that one issue has impacted me more than the other, but what I can say is that raising a Black Male with an Intellectual Disability is my greatest challenge and my most fulfilling assignment.

I am the mother of three children. My only son, Nicholas, has Down syndrome. This disability affects how he learns, moves, and regulates his emotions, and causes him to struggle with activities that his twin sister and other typical children his age find easy to master. This disability also puts him at risk for certain medical conditions such as heart defects, respiratory and hearing problems, Alzheimer's disease, childhood leukemia, and thyroid conditions. All people with Down syndrome experience cognitive delays; however, social and community integration allows their competence to override their differences. Some other commonalities are found in facial structures such as a flattened nose, broad short hands with a single crease in the palm, short fingers, protruding tongue, excessive flexibility, and a wide gap between the first and second toe. I feel the need to point out that none of these "differences" are immediately seen in my son. My Black son.

Setbacks and uncertainties are the major source of the pain my heart feels for my son. Growing up in a world that is not designed to accept his differences readily. My truth is that along with monitoring his heart health, learning how to teach him to effectively communicate his needs, building independence, advocating for acceptance, and demanding inclusion—he is still seen as a Black Boy growing into a man that is, in essence, an endangered species. How disheartening it is, knowing that as hard as he works to be normal, his life is not as valuable as his peers.

Nicholas will have developmental delays for his entire life, and for the rest of my own life, I will be dedicated to advocating for him to be treated fairly. This genetic disability results in him being as defective as medical science could predict. This means that I also get to watch his disabilities cause him to struggle with simple tasks, not understand complex requests, be excluded from events with his typical peers, struggle to keep up with his twin and be left behind by those who notice his differences.

Not only do I get to raise Nicholas, but I also have two daughters who need me. In my opinion, this is a high-level assignment that society doesn't always support. I grew up believing that life would offer me the fairytale that Cinderella and Sleeping Beauty lived, but that is not so. With the current social media craze, we can get caught up in the "look" of things and will end up realizing that looks can be deceiving.

I've been told to lower my expectations of my son as a means of not feeling like he was unsuccessful. But I choose to look at him as a seed. With seeds, there is a time for planting, cultivating, watering, nurturing, helping to mature, and feeding—all while roots are being established. Have you ever looked at a root? A root starts thick and gradually gets thinner, and the thinner part is able to go deeper. Established roots are needed to protect and provide nourishment to the growing buds. That makes me believe that we have to let go of the non-essential things in our lives, such as hatred toward others who are not akin to us. We cannot continue to believe that our answer is the only answer or the only correct answer when others face conditions and disabilities that we may not know about.

My son has a diagnosed genetic disability, but we all have something that disables us from being loving human beings to all people. We must concern ourselves with being like a root—reaching out to gather nutrients needed to supply our families, our children, and our neighbors. Like a root—everything does not have to be exposed. It's in the quiet and private times that we spend learning about ourselves that we can see ourselves in the purest form. We must strip away the non-essential desires that we have and remember that GOD writes the game plan.

Seeds grow in areas that are bigger than the seed, and it also must have some good soil. I looked at my own life and realized that Nicholas, with all of his developmental delays and differences, has been well-positioned in our family. He is surrounded by a Village of relatives and friends that are retired and current educators. They make up the soil for his healthy existence. He is also positioned in life with a twin sister and an older sister…so now what?

So now, I consider the soil…

If you ever plant a seed and it does not grow, you don't remove the seed; you change the conditions of the soil. Soil conditioners are soil amendments that improve the soil structure so that the seed does not experience an issue or a combination of issues. Without proper soil, the seed cannot survive. This has been the same approach I've attempted to use when considering the society that my family, especially my son, is living in. The world's soil is contaminated. As I have tried to increase awareness and educate others about the myths that are exaggerated regarding those with disabilities, I have faced discrimination that I would have never imagined.

People who are different in any manner are discriminated against or bullied in some shape, form, or fashion. Unfortunately, my experience has been that even within the outcasted group, there is still discrimination if the color of your skin is Black. I've experienced the racial injustice in smaller community groups as well as on the National level.

Once I fully accepted the cards life dealt me, I began my journey of trying to improve the conditions of the soil my son is buried in, so that he can grow, thrive, and offer his best into society while being treated equally.

Social media was my starting point. I began sharing pictures and stories about my children, and most people began to comment on Nicholas, and how "normal" he seemed to be, as if they didn't expect normalcy from him. They would comment on how well he looked, acted, and eventually spoke. It began to register with me that there are people who have little to no expectancy of those who are different. This ultimately propelled me into wanting to uncover and expose how similar we are, even when we carry situations that disable us, or the color of our skin makes us look different.

I began to seek and connect to other parents whose children were older than my son in hopes that I could get some useful tips along this journey. Additionally, I had returned to school to complete my studies and ultimately had some work published. Through one of the publications, a woman reached out to me, who also has a son with Down syndrome. Her son was older than mine, and they were Black. She immediately captured my attention simply by the dynamics of her family. We were able to chat, and I quickly realized that she was already advocating for her son, and I needed to do the same. After many conversations and suggestions, I was introduced to a national organization that I had never heard of before. This was strange to me since my son was four years old and was born with his genetic disability. By the urging of my new friend, I joined the group.

As I began to participate in workshops and study all mailers and electronic articles, I noticed the faces of color were missing. We were not represented in parent groups, articles of hope, nor videos. Who would be a voice for the concerns for my child? This was my reality check! That even when you have the same disability as your peer—there is still discrimination. I decided to do my part in bringing our face of color and voice to the table. For two years, I was accepted and invited to teach workshops during the National Convention. There, I offered a voice of hope and a level of understanding that parents and teachers could understand and appreciate. My feedback and reviews from the participants were excellent. I was a new face; I did what I was asked to do. I was informative, encouraging, relatable, and inspiring—all of the prerequisites. Even in the workshops, I noticed that I could count how many African Americans were in attendance on one hand and have a few fingers left. But that didn't matter to me because I was willing to be that token negro if it meant we were represented.

I did have the opportunity to meet an older African American woman one year who was accompanied by her husband and grown son with Down syndrome. Immediately our hearts connected, and I felt like the baton was being passed to me because she was tired---tired of being that "one" who had to represent the entire culture within that community of differently-abled individuals. My heart hurt for her because I could just imagine all the inequalities she had lived through within her generation---I silently vowed to keep fighting for her Black son and mine.

She had a smile of pride mixed with compassion as the sound man began to connect my microphone. Pride, because "one of us" is in front now to tell our story, and compassion, because she knew better than I did what discrimination I would face from the same organization that let me in.

I taught my workshop for this organization for two years with good feedback from the attendants. Being a parent, I could relate to the questions and concerns each one had, and being a Minister, I would encourage their faith and pray for those who requested. The total package, so I thought. What I would end up learning is that the things that make you stand-out can be the same things that hold you back.

I was accepted when I raised money to support the organization's effort when the national convention was hosted in my city. I made several trips to churches, restaurants, fraternal organizations, and community partners to collect products needed for childcare so that parents could attend the various workshops without the responsibility of bringing their child with them. I felt like I had found my place, my tribe, those who understood things that I didn't have the words to express.

However, after three years, I was denied the opportunity to speak. Not because of feedback from attendees, not because of missing any deadlines, not because of the workshop outline…but because of the "title" of my workshop, which is the title of one of my published books, "Winning With a Losing Hand." I was told that it was "too controversial." The decision and explanation came in an email to make sure I could not challenge the reasoning. What a slap in the face! I was made to feel like I'm good enough for the behind the scenes work, but not to stay at the forefront. I felt like my voice and demand for equal treatment for my son and all the Black sons and daughters that will come behind him was being silenced, as if we were not important enough.

What they do not know is that I am not a quitter, and I will never model a "give up" behavior to my children. I choose to wear my truths like an exquisite necklace rather than like a noose. Black lives matter, even when some may think that because it's a disabled life, it's a lesser quality. It's instances like this that make me more aggressive in my advocacy efforts. It's like my son has been given a double dose of shame—disabled and Black. My truth is, I do have to teach him how to Win With a Losing Hand! I refuse to sit on the sidelines and not make sure that predominantly White institutions of change don't have a burst of color. Everyone doesn't speak the same language, nor do we comprehend the same. I know how to talk to and speak up for my people, and that's what I intend to do.

This setback has been what has prompted me to find other ways of getting my voice heard within the differently-abled community. It is my desire that more parents of color will begin to demand their seat at the table and fight for equal rights for their children. Equality cannot be attained until every human being, regardless of their IQ or functioning level, is treated equally based on their need. Equality cannot be equalized or leveled. Everyone does not need the same thing. Equality says, "I will give you the things you need so that we are on the same level ground." Some of us may need more assistance than others.

I share my story so that others will feel empowered to share theirs also. I share my story because my Black son has Down syndrome and his life matters. He does not understand racial tension, setback, and inequality. He doesn't understand the impact of his mother's voice being silenced at a time when it's needed most. But he has taught me to have strong faith, and it is my belief that God will open up a pathway to be invited in to speak to others—from the Black perspective—but when they are ready to truly hear me.

Proverbs 31:8-9 (NIV)

"Speak up for those who cannot speak for themselves, for the rights of all who are destitute. Speak up and judge fairly; defend the rights of the poor and needy."

About Dr. Anita

Dr. Anita A. Penn enjoys empowering and inspiring individuals of all ages and walks of life to get out of their comfort zone and take a front-row seat in life!

In 2009, Anita accepted the challenge to become a stay at home mom to her three children Nadia, Nia, and Nicholas. The demanding special medical needs that came along with her son Nicholas is what ultimately caused her bold confession to "trust, lean, and maximize her relationship with her Savior"—and the calling to ministry was birthed within her.

Anita is a graduate of Jarvis Christian College of Hawkins, TX, and earned her Master's and Ph.D. in Urban Ministries from Aspen Christian College and Seminary of Aspen, CO. She gained her Christian Life Coach Certification and Professional Life Coach Certification from New Life Coach, Inc.

Anita is the author of Discipling Through Your Disability, where she shares the beginning of her journey with her son Nicholas who has Down syndrome and CHD. Her most recent book, Winning With A Losing Hand, leaves readers considering strategies for making the best out of unfavorable circumstances of life.

Anita is the founder of Just In The Nic of Time Ministries and "In My Aunties Arms" 501(c)(3) non-profit organization. Her passions lie in empowering and encouraging others not to lose their faith when faced with major life-changing events. Most recently, she has begun coaching her son's basketball team with the Special Olympics of TX, where he affectionately calls her the "Fake Coach"!

You can find Anita, also known as "Dr. Auntie," weeknights on Facebook Live hosting "9@9", where at 9 pm (CST), she shares 9 minutes of thought-provoking words of encouragement to women from all walks of life.

For more information and to join our journey, please visit www.iamdrauntie.org

Chapter 11
"A Delayed Lesson"

By Nikki Lewis Willis

Growing up in South Louisiana, well, you expect to see a little bit of everything. You see, Louisiana has a full cultural spectrum of people. You have your whites, blacks, creole, a few Frenchmen, and the rest would be called lagniappe. With such a substantial population of people in the mid-'80s, you would think that everyone was getting along. Louisiana is best known for its food, music, and love of a festival. These three seem to mend and bring people together at all times. Oh, did I forget to mention the drinks? You can walk up to any festival and find people from all walks of life, eating, drinking, and dancing together. Hey, I have even heard it said that people from Louisiana always have a change of party clothes in the car.

So, you can see how growing up as a young black girl in South Louisiana could be a lot of fun. I come from a bonded family, so I loved being a kid in Louisiana. With so much family support, I have always felt that I could do anything I put my mind to and follow through. That so led me to believe I could speak my mind also. Now, that part kept me in trouble. But, with my family growing up, fear was not a thing I learned at an early age. Fear of someone because of the color of their skin was not on the table for this little loudmouth girl.

Let me get on with the story. One day in late September while riding with my mom and aunt in Hammond, LA, the crazy thing happened. I can't remember the purpose of the trip. I'm sure there was some shopping involved. What I do remember is that it was cool enough for us to have the windows rolled down and the radio on. There was a lot of talking and laughing going on in the car. My mom was driving, while my aunt was in the passenger front seat and me in the back. As we pulled up and stopped at the red light, a Jeep Wrangler pulled up to the right of us. In this Jeep were three young white males. I would say they may have been in their early or mid-twenties. I guess life seems to be going too well for us because out of nowhere, the one in the passenger seat of the Jeep looked over and boldly called us some dirty niggers. My mom turned and looked at him, and he spits at her. At that point, the light turned green, and an army of words went back and forth.

My mom pulled over in the closest parking lot, which was a Wendy's. She got out of the car to go inside and clean her face. These young men pull over in the parking lot as well. I can only guess they had more to say. By this time, my aunt had gotten out of the car, opened the trunk, and pulled out a lug wrench. I can only assume she was not about to change a tire for them. As I stood beside her, ready to go all-in with her, others took notice.

Two older men that were across the street from the bank's parking lot came over to see if they could help. At the same time, one black man in Wendy's parking walked up with a bat. You know what I thought was just wrong; that the older people around me knew the deep-rooted disrespect that was coming from those young men. Whereas the black man came to stand and fight with my aunt, the other two white men came to stop the whole thing altogether.

They told those three white boys to get back in their truck and go back to where they came from. They told them that around here, we don't do things like that. Around here, we have peace and that if they step back and allow this fight to break out, lives may be lost. When they asked the young men what happened, they said it was just the sight of three niggers laughing and that we had no reason to laugh. I remember one of the older white men laughing and putting his hand on his hips and saying to them. "Son, you all gone run up on a hell of a whooping down here in Louisiana thinking like that." The driver of the Jeep said, "That's the problem now. You have allowed blacks to think we are their friends; they need to know their place."

At this point, my aunt began to tell them where their place in life was, and her words were full of color, while she hit their Jeep. The other two white men that came to help told them to get back in their Jeep and leave. By this time, my mom was walking back out, and let's say she was madder than an alligator whose dinner had been interrupted.

She was ready to go all in!

They were convinced to leave and go about their way. But they did not leave before letting us know that a few cities over, they were headed to a meeting where blacks could not come. He told her that their Grand was about to make changes in our parts so that niggers would know how to act.

Well, as you can imagine, our trip was cut short, and we headed back home. That car ride was quiet, and things seemed out of place. Later that night, my mom talked with me about the events of the day. She wanted to know how I felt. I told her I was mad and would have felt better if I hit them. I went on and on about all the things I wanted to do to them. She never said a word, so I asked her, "How did it make you feel." She looked at me and said, "Afraid. Afraid that people like that want to hurt me for merely laughing and enjoying my day." She was afraid that if she were not there, I would not know to walk away and get help. She told me that every battle is not to be fought. There is a war to win---hang around for the war. I must have been all of twelve at that time. That made no sense to me.

Now, here in my mid-forties with two black sons of my own, I understand it 100%. I tell my sons that it's okay, and better, to walk away from a battle, and you will see who's still standing for the war.

About Nikki

Nikki G.L. Willis is the owner of Adore New Credit. She spent over 20 years in corporate accounting. She is known by her peers for always helping and giving information on how to build and fix credit.

Nikki's goals now are to help others in their journey to financial freedom. With rebuilding, restoring credit, and creating clear business plans, others will be able to see retirement, travel, and enjoy the life they have dreamed about. The goal is while on the journey to a life of freedom, bring others along with me so I'll have friends to enjoy life with.

In her free time, she loves to dance, especially Chicago Stepping.

She is a wife and mother of 3. She and her family reside in Grand Prairie, Texas.

Chapter 12
"Building Wealth, Education, Mentorship, and Allyship"

By LaDeitra Lee

As both COVID-19 and protests over the death of George Floyd have been declared a pandemic in the black community, I am glad that I have the opportunity to share the racial injustice I have experienced and witnessed. I'm LaDeitra (AKA DeDe) and grew up in Memphis, TN, where the racial composition of the community is Black/African American: 64.22%, White: 29.08%, Other race: 3.36%, Two or more races: 1.57%, Asian: 1.56% (according to World Population Review). I attended schools that serviced over 98% black students throughout elementary, middle school, and high school in the Whitehaven area, which is now informally known as Blackhaven, which was a more predominantly white area before the 1970s.

My parents were teachers at predominantly white schools in MS, where they grew up. Although we lived in Memphis, my parents did not teach there because they wanted to work with people they grew up with, people they already had a great relationship with, knew, and loved them, most of which were allies. My parents grew up in schools that were still segregated. They were raised and taught to be kind and respectful to all people and never blatantly treat other races badly. They were aware, just as we are aware of our differences and how uncomfortable whites were (that did not know us) while in our presence.

I attended a Historically Black College and University (HBCU), Jackson State University (JSU) located in Jackson,

MS, where my father also graduated. JSU today services over 91% of black students. I played volleyball on a full athletic scholarship. My white basketball coach, who was an amazing ally, more like a mom, took me to JSU to try out and then talked to the coach about making my scholarship possible. That--I was blessed with! Being in a huge black community felt like a big family to me.

Teachers were more like my aunts and uncles who would call home if things were not going well for me at school. Thankfully, I did not have that problem, but some students did because we were all treated like family. We ensured that no student that was truly working hard to succeed in college would be left behind.

I never honestly thought about the demographics around me as a child. I loved my child's upbringing, college experience, and the love and support I received from my predominantly black community as I excelled in academics and sports. It was not until I was removed from my "black bubble" that I felt that I was truly a minority and that I was viewed differently in America. I soon experienced racial discrimination more so while trying to find an internship in technology. I was not amongst those getting internships the summer right after their sophomore year of college, although I had several interviews. This was the time I first felt that I was not enough and that I was defeated.

I did not let that stop me from continuing to interview and search for co-op/internship experience. I remained determined to be the best student I could be, praying several times a day for that 1st offer to put my Computer Science Learnings to work. During the 1st semester of my Junior year of college, I received my 1st internship/co-op job offer as a Computer Science student in Fort Meade, Maryland, followed by another opportunity in Raleigh, North Carolina. It was those times in my life that I had experienced many 1sts such as; first time on an airplane, the first time being the only black or amongst 2% of blacks in a training, job, orientation, work event, project, assignment, or community. I often felt isolated and quite different from all the other students. Being in this environment is when I could remember being harassed by a police officer when I was pulled over. Still, my more serious experiences of feeling that I was discriminated against came later in my career as I moved into people management.

In 1999, I experienced harsh treatment by police officers who pulled my husband and me over one late night/early morning during a 9-hour drive from Austin, Texas (where my husband and I have resided since 2000); we were headed to Jackson, Mississippi (where we met in college in the computer lab at JSU) for JSU's Homecoming. Because of the horror stories my husband and I have heard and seen on TV of how things have turned out for blacks in America when being pulled over by the police, we both would get extremely scared, upset, irritated, and nervous when a policeman pulls us over. Twice, my husband, a young black man, has been pulled over. Instead of just having to show his license and registration, he was commanded by the police officer to get out of the car and open his trunk to show items he was traveling with. He was questioned for over an hour and asked if they could put the police dogs in the car so they could search it. My husband and I felt that this was because we were young, fresh out of college, black, and riding in a genuinely nice car.

Being very educated, calm, corresponding to the officer's orders, and aware of our rights, I stayed in the car on the passenger side, raging with fear and worry. At the same time, my husband got out of the car and answered the police officer's questions calmly, but one could tell he was annoyed and angry. More officers came on the scene after my husband refused to let the police dogs in our car, now having three officers (all white men) interrogating us on the side of the road in Louisiana. The first officer questioned me again, while the second officer questioned my husband again, and while the third officer ran the police dog around our car. This was during the time of pagers and no cell phones, so nothing was being recorded, no ticket was given, and thankfully the situation did not escalate further.

Having come from a family of police officers where my stepdaughter is a police officer in Jackson, MS, and my brother and sister-in-law are officers in Memphis, TN, we have been drilled many times on how to interact with police officers and, no matter what the situation, to never run, reach for anything, and always be respectful in tone, behavior, and voice. This extremely upsets the police officer if we appear disrespectful, in turn, causing the officer to become angry and act out of character as an officer.

This is not to say that those that may react in such a way deserve to be shot and killed. Sadly, we have seen white Americans kill people in mass shootings, and they still make it out of the situation alive. But, far too often, we see black Americans killed by police during police interactions.

I quickly learned that when a civilian commits a crime or breaks the law, they are generally arrested, tried, and then convicted. When a black civilian commits a crime, they are usually treated as though they are already convicted immediately, as they are when pulled over by the police. Even when there is a lot of evidence, it is very rare to secure an indictment against a police officer for excessive force. And an indictment is just a trial; it is not a conviction. If something did get out of control and the situation escalated, it would be very unlikely this would turn out in our favor.

My husband and I teach our young children (ages 17, 13, 11) that if any of them are pulled over by the police to remember to be calm, patient, respectful, and transparent to ensure they return to their families unharmed after the incident. We teach our kids the statistics show that black Americans remain 2.5 times as likely to die at the hands of police (ref: www.statista.com/chart/21872/map-of-police-violence-against-black-americans/) and be looked over for high positions in the workplace or employment when compared to white Americans because of systemic racism (ref: https://www.businessinsider.com/us-systemic-racism-in-charts-graphs-data-2020-6). Black Americans are five times as likely to be fatally shot by a police officer than as a white American (ref: https://www.bbc.com/news/world-us-canada-52877678).

When it was time to decide where we wanted to live, my husband and I decided, as Software Engineers, we would move to Austin, Texas, where the racial composition of the community is White: 73.49%, Black or African American: 7.84%, Other race: 7.47%, Asian: 7.33%, Two or more races: 3.25% (according to World Population Review).

Given all of the available statistics, facts, and learnings, my husband and I chose to raise our kids in predominantly white areas. Not because they were mostly white, but because they all had exceptional ratings, low crime, and many opportunities for high tech professionals. These areas have better schools. Over 98% of the kids are meeting the scores in Math and Reading, making these public schools exemplary. We wanted our kids to have better facilities, learning environments, tools, resources, and higher education without the burden of paying fees for private schools.

Although we do not regret making this choice, there have been challenges for our children, such as feeling like they do not belong because they look different due to their hair and skin color. My daughter has been one of the 1 or 2 black girls in her grade each year for her entire elementary studies. She had her Indian classmates think that she was Indian because of her dark skin because they had never experienced having an African American classmate.

One day her dad went to the school to have lunch with her. Her Indian classmate kept staring at them. He kept looking at her, then her dad, then back at her, then her dad again. Finally, he said, “I thought you were Indian.”

Many of her classmates often touch and pull her hair because they are amazed at how different it is from theirs. She has been called bossy because she is noticeably confident and a natural-born leader. She is very comfortable in her uniqueness and aware of her strengths, often helping her classmates and raising her hand to participate in class, or leading groups when they have small group activities in class.

One of my sons experienced being chased in the neighborhood by all of his white "friends" with BB guns only to finally be saved by another African American neighbor who heard the commotion and pulled my son into their house. They immediately called me to tell me what was going on after they spoke with the kids. They asked them if they think that this is nice how they are treating him. They said, "I don't know." The neighbor asked, "Well, would you like being chased by four boys firing BBs at you?" They stood there shy and embarrassed, replying, "No."

This same son, as he grew older, participated in triathlons, swimming year-round, running cross-country, and playing water polo, football, and basketball. He experienced having to go to cross country practice each day and getting up at 5 am to make it to a 6 am practice, only to be called nigger by one of his teammates as he ran past him during the workout. As my husband and I shared this with friends, we also learned of a black girl at the school, who picked up her artwork at the end of the school year and noticed that someone wrote nigger all over her work.

Some sports only have about 2% blacks; therefore, my husband and I have tried to expose our kids to all sports, so they will not ever feel like they are not equipped or equally experienced as their white friends. My daughter has been sidelined and not given opportunities in volleyball although she was stronger and better than her white teammate. She had to experience teammates making racist comments, like stating that she must also play basketball because of her black skin. She told her coach, only for the coach to tell her she should take it as a compliment.

My family and I believe as Dr. Martin Luther King, Jr. stated, “I have a dream that my four little children will one day live in a nation where they will not be judged by the color of their skin, but by the content of their character.” I believe that before Black Lives Matter and Trump taking office, some of the cruel things people say to each other today in 2020 would have never come up directly to a black person’s face. Today, more people seem to speak loudly about their racist, prejudiced views without shame. All of these things are sad, but the good thing is, once we spoke to the school administration, neighbors, as well as other parents, behaviors like this lessened, and all three of our children have thoroughly enjoyed being raised in Austin (Round Rock), TX. They have wonderful friends of all different races and economic backgrounds that have become closer, I feel, as a result of Black Lives Matter and George Floyd’s death.

Their sports teammates had reached out to them to discuss how they each were feeling and how they can be allies. We have had several neighbor allies protest with us and speak up on our behalf and allow us to share our experience of racial injustice with the neighbors to help end racial injustice, police brutality, discrimination, hate, and racism by educating one another, talking about all history, white and black people history.

Racial injustice does not just happen at home and in the schools; it happens in the workplace. How black employees see racism at work depends on the job title/role/position. I believe that the reason you do not see many Blacks in higher positions like Director, VP, SVP, CEO, and CIO, is because we do not have enough people who look like us in the workplace. Studies show that everyone has biases and naturally wants to work with, collaborate, and network with those that look and think as they do. I believe that I have experienced biases in hiring, performance ratings, and promotions.

I have worked extremely hard as a Leader in Software Engineering. My white counterparts could not do half of what I am doing and yet receive a higher rating or promotion. White employees could also make critical errors in their work and still be rewarded with a higher rating, award, bonus, or pay. However, if a black employee were to make the same mistake, they would be written up and put on a performance plan.

Black employees have been taught by their parents to prepare for issues like this, as they often arise in our community. These differences are linked to positions in the organizational hierarchy. Higher status in an organization means more exposure to how policies and rules are made and the impact those can have on black employees across the organization.

I experienced being sidelined when I shared innovation and process improvement ideas. My ideas were directed to be carried out by my white male peer instead of by me. I also felt unappreciated and devalued in Corporate America. There have been times when I had to pitch a roadmap or process improvement to an audience, that instead of giving respect and paying attention, decided to look at their phones or do other things. While presenting my data and pitching my findings and research to a room of white Americans and Asians, I was given the death stare and often rudely interrupted. I believe that all of these unprofessional and disrespectful behaviors were meant to hurt me and to push me to quit, but instead, they fueled and intrigued me. I continue in my role to win them over, woo them, and befriend my enemies. As the old saying goes, “Keep your friends close and your enemies closer.”

While black/African Americans and other people of color comprise 36% of the overall U.S. workforce, we constitute 58% of miscellaneous agricultural workers; 70% of maids and housekeeping cleaners; and 74% of baggage porters, bellhops, and concierges. (ref: ttps://www.americanprogress .org/issues/race/reports/2019/08/07/472910/systematic-

-inequality-economic-opportunity/)

Slavery and Jim Crow devalued these types of jobs, and the legacy of these institutions continue to hold us back from moving forward. Our opportunity to build wealth, education, mentorship, allyship, and a legacy for our children, has been robbed from us by racial injustices, prejudice, and brainwashing in America. Black/African Americans still battle every day with this mindset that we are not enough, we are not smart enough, or we can't possibly fill that high position in that organization. We go and get all the college degrees that we can afford (or not afford). We go into more debt, to prove to ourselves and white Americans that we belong here, that we can be on their level, and that we are educated enough for them to trust us and give us the opportunity, by hiring and promoting us. It's not enough for black/African Americans to go to college and get a degree. We must strive for putting ourselves in jobs, roles, and leadership positions where we are under-represented. It is these positions that will help us build the wealth and education that was stolen from us all of these years. It saddens me that still today, the majority of black/African Americans go after jobs that are domestic servitude and lowest-paid.

Not only are we filling the lowest-paid jobs, but we are also lost because we don't know our ancestors, and we don't have a family inheritance or life insurance payouts passed down to us. You don't see us as stay-at-home parents. Instead, both parents work to save and invest as much money as we can, as we are still trying to catch up; due to the wealth we tried to build with communities and learning that our ancestors were not afforded and given the opportunity to be a family, as black/African Americans are today. The past and present hurt so deep that I often lose sleep. I strive each day to ensure that my kids learn black/African American history and that they love the skin they're in and the hair "crown" they are so blessed with as we were built to stand out from the crowd.

Many things we were taught came from a slave mentality. Many experiences we have had, we had no idea were wrong or racial injustices because it was our way of life. We stayed in the place our parents and grandparents taught us to ensure happiness, and that we got to live to see the next day. Some upbringings that we were taught, like saying "yes ma'am, no ma'am," seems to stem from slavery and Jim Crow days. "If you didn't say 'yes, sir' or 'no, sir,' you were going to get 40 lashes from your master as they mandated respect. As a child, I was taught by my parents, grandparents, teachers, and other elders to always say sir or ma'am when speaking to an adult. Any omission of these manners was considered disrespectful. It made parents look bad when their children didn't show these manners to adults. It's something that many black/African Americans were taught, and even as adults, we still use these terms to honor older family members, show that we still have manners, and we ensure our children show the same courtesy.

Today, with the death of George Floyd, Black Lives Matter, and continuous reports of black people dying at the hands of police, and other racist people, I try to teach myself the history I was never taught. History about my ancestors, their struggles, the many racial injustices, systemic racism, and the way of life we had to get by, day to day. Several stones meant to be buried forever have been turned. The U.S. economy was built on the exploitation and occupational segregation of black/African Americans.

Thanks to Speaker/Author/Civil Rights Activist Kimberly Latrice Jones' video shared on June 6, 2020, I learned about two places in America that massive massacres of black people happened in and were partially covered up over the years: Rosewood and Tulsa. I was thrilled to read on Wikipedia about "Black Wall Street" in Tulsa and devastated at the same time to know it was destroyed in a racist attack. "Before the massacre, the town of Rosewood had been a quiet, primarily black, self-sufficient whistle stop on the Seaboard Air Line Railway. Trouble began when white men from several nearby towns lynched a black Rosewood resident because of accusations that a white woman in nearby Sumner had been assaulted by a black drifter." — Wikipedia

Wikipedia describes Rosewood as a place with no enemies. A quiet town of people who just wanted to live in peace. As you'll see later on, though, the story of 'a white woman being assaulted by a black man' has been used by white people to enact violence against black people.

"No arrests were made for what happened in Rosewood. The town was abandoned by its former black and white residents; none ever moved back, and the town ceased to exist." — Wikipedia

The Tulsa race massacre (also called the Tulsa race riot, the Greenwood Massacre, or the Black Wall Street Massacre) took place on May 31 and June 1, 1921, when mobs of white residents attacked black residents and businesses of the Greenwood District in Tulsa, Oklahoma.[1] It has been called "the single worst incident of racial violence in American history."[15] The attack, carried out on the ground and from private aircraft, destroyed more than 35 square blocks of the district — at that time the wealthiest black community in the United States, known as "Black Wall Street." — Wikipedia

"The massacre began over Memorial Day weekend after 19-year-old Dick Rowland, a black shoe shiner, was accused of assaulting Sarah Page, the 17-year-old white elevator operator of the nearby Drexel Building." — Wikipedia

These two events are an outrage! Like Kimberly Latrice Jones cries out in her June 6, 2020 video, "we don't own anything!" This is why building wealth, education, mentorship, and allyship within and for the black community, and putting melanated faces in high places is strongly encouraged today. I hope this is not only popular for today but remains the acts and courtesy of tomorrow.

To lower the risk of being heavily affected by systemic racism and discrimination, my husband and I continue to educate ourselves, families, and circle of friends about investing and not just saving, teaching various ways to build wealth and ownership to ensure we leave behind a great legacy. My husband and I are both managers in the Information Technology (IT) industry, extremely committed to philanthropy and giving back to the community in poverty-stricken areas, the homeless, and youth seeking careers in IT.

About LaDeitra

LaDeitra's (AKA DeDe) passion for helping others began as a child. For over 28 years, she has devoted her life to motivating and coaching athletes, engineers, women, and other IT professionals. When she heard about Deidre's desire to start the work, "Black Women Speak Out: Stories Of Racial Injustice In America," to bring more awareness and solutions to racism, discrimination, police brutality, and other injustices, she jumped in immediately.

LaDeitra currently serves as Vice President/Social Media Lead of non-profit, Ladders for Leaders. She is also an active member of Austin Women in Tech, Austin Alumnae Chapter of Delta Sigma Theta Sorority, Inc., Board Member of Jamsz Konnections, National Society of Black Engineers, National Black MBA Association and in the past, has served as the National President of Sisters Tri-ing Health and Fitness Group, Inc. and Founder of the Austin Chapter, as well as other community impacting organizations such as American Diabetes Association, Black Professional Alliance, Livestrong, and Helping Hands-Austin, and Blanket Statement of Love. LaDeitra continues to empower others to be unapologetically the best version of themselves.

LaDeitra holds a BS in Computer Science from Jackson State University where she received a full volleyball scholarship and was the team captain for two years. She is a full-time Sr. Team Manager of Software Development and Engineering at Charles Schwab Corporation.

Some of her most memorable accomplishments include being one of six of Charles Schwab Corporation's 2019

Outstanding Community Service Award Recipients, being a Keynote Speaker for BA Women's Alliance EmpowHER, completing the Livestrong 100 Mile Century Ride in the fight for a cancer cure, and her participation in Tour de Cure of Central Texas in the fight for a diabetes cure. She is excited to bring her wealth of experience as a Contributing Author of the work, "Black Women Speak Out: Stories Of Racial Injustice In America."

She's a wife, mother, daughter, triathlete, cyclist, and past marathon runner.

You can find her on LinkedIn under LaDeitra Lee.

Chapter 13
"Relationships that Challenge Change"

By LaVal Ezell

I was born and raised in Little Rock, Arkansas, in which I am the oldest of four children. My mother and father made sure that my siblings and I experienced life inside and outside the black community. It was my father that led our family in loving God's Word through the traditional black Baptist Church and introduced us to the Nondenominational Church experience. We learned more about ourselves and God through both experiences. As an adult, I treasure both experiences.

My mother was one of the few black women in Arkansas to be trained as a Montessori School teacher in the '80s. She and her friend were willing to get out of their comfort zone to advance their teaching career, which was untraditional. I was able to attend Montessori School, where my mother worked, which was a predominantly white community. I enjoyed the opportunity that the private school had to offer, and I made friends that didn't look like me. One of my best friends in elementary had freckles and red hair, and I enjoyed getting to know her and her family. My friendship with her and other girls that didn't look like me sparked a new type of friendship that would be very diverse as I grew older. I was curious about having different types of friendships. My adult friendships have been diversely cultivated due to experiencing diversity at an early age.

I attended the historical Little Rock Central High which was segregated in 1957, so I understood the history of desegregation. I loved our school pride at Central High, which was demonstrated by all races, but our school couldn't get away from the negative media press due to the student body being predominantly black. We were in the heart of the black community, and we celebrated our heritage and traditions in many ways. During my senior year, we had our annual homecoming parade in which a racial riot broke out among the students. As a result, students were running and screaming everywhere. All you could hear was screaming, with police on horses and police cars surrounding the school.

That experience was very traumatic for me. It made me feel like it was like 1957 again! Yet the best black experience in high school was being a part of the African play, Shaka Zulu. It was an amazing experience when I realized confidence and pride in my African roots. During the summers, I attended Upward Bound, which influenced me to see the world globally. I remember learning the Black National Anthem song, "Lift Every Voice and Sing," one summer during Upward Bound at Philander Smith College in Little Rock. We were given an opportunity to celebrate and express our black heritage in many ways during that time, and I loved it!

I moved to Texas and began to experience a new level of diversity. I first lived in the cultural melting pot of Dallas for many years. I also was a member of a predominantly black mega ministry in Dallas for over ten years. I met my husband there through a mutual friend. Then once married, we moved north of Dallas. The first city we lived in was slowly growing in diversity, so I would notice a few blacks in the city. Living in this city was a new season for our family, so we were determined to make the best of it! When you're black and live in a city where the population is predominantly white, it's like all eyes are on you wherever you go. You get looks like, "Do you belong here"?

During this time, I was a stay at home mom, and most people were not used to seeing a black mom during storytime at the library, playing with kids at the local park, or hanging at the mall in the middle of the day. Even in the black community, being a stay at home mom was uncommon and can be undervalued because most black women don't have the opportunity to experience it. As blacks, we didn't see it being done because most families can't afford to have one income. I became a stay at home mom by accident when I was laid off in 2004 and was pregnant with my 3rd child. My husband had a desire for me to stay home and care for our family. I thank God for his willingness to work hard for our family. The eleven years at home with my children were the best years of my life in motherhood. It was a sacrifice in the area of not having some luxuries, but it was worth it to stay home with my children, create memories, and watch them develop. As a black woman, I didn't understand the value of staying in the home, but now I do! I thank God for blessing us with that gift.

God opened an opportunity for us to purchase our first home in another city with a smaller ratio of blacks in the community. This house was a blessing for our family, but the city was concerning because of how rural it was at the time. We always lived in the city, and now all I could see was cornfields and tractors. I had a bit of fear of the unknown living in this city due to the historical acronym that the black community knew of the city name...ANNA. Which stood for: Ain't No Niggers Allowed. So, moving to this city was awkward and frightening because I knew that we were a minority, and I wasn't sure what to expect. I didn't want to expect the worst, so I looked for the positive side. It was much different than what I was used to in the larger city. I was determined to make it home.

As a family, we wanted to be of value to our new community. I remember going to the grocery store and not seeing anyone that looked like me. I knew that I would have to be friendlier than normal so that others wouldn't feel awkward around me. So, I was determined to extend my friendliest attributes. Living in this rural city was a bit uncomfortable because usually, I was the only black woman in the room or event. We put forth an effort to connect and participate in local functions and community events. Living in my city was a little fearful in many ways because of the unknown of the dark roads and the mindset of people or police in the community. When you don't see many of your own race in a community, it can feel troublesome.

As time went on, I learned to get to know the person's heart and not just see the color of their skin and assume. Our family and friends questioned the choice of our homestead, but I knew God opened doors for us in this unfamiliar city. As we lived in this community, we experienced a variety of things. Our children started school, and we connected with the local Boy scouts Troop. In school, my children were usually the only black students in the classroom from first grade to fifth grade. Most teachers were very surprised when they met my son, who is very mild-mannered, very intelligent, and talented for his age. The teachers would always tell me, "Oh my gosh, your son is wonderful," “He's always so helpful,” in a surprised voice. I felt that most white teachers in the community had not experienced this in black boys. Therefore, it was like a miracle or something. As a black mother, I thought, what did they expect?

We joined the local Boy Scouts group. We were the only black family, and a few Hispanic families participated in Cub Scouts. Therefore, it was a bit awkward at first. The troop leaders welcomed our family. My son loved camping, and I was determined to help him participate in camping. I was very nervous about camping as the only black mom in this atmosphere, but I embraced the uncharted experience. My husband was not an outdoorsman and usually had to work, so I learned to rough it through camping out. Their dad was impressed that I could set up a tent and create a camp space. It was one of those experiences my dad gave me, so I was not totally lost. The troop was supportive and trained us to endure the grueling cold camping experience. This was a positive experience, but we got looks from some dads like, what are you all doing here, or they didn't know what to expect from us. Once again, we always went the extra yard to be friendly and approachable. When it comes to life, we must seek to understand one another.

Living in my community has created an opportunity for me to develop authentic relationships with White and Hispanic women in a personable way. I was unfamiliar with the Hispanic culture, and I had no close white female friends, only acquaintances. My Hispanic neighbor became my sister from another mother. Our children were inseparable because we raised them together and built a strong bond. We learned so much from one another. If it had not been for my experience and connection with her, I might not have enjoyed this new city. Relationships make a major difference in our lives. Our bond was so strong, and I treasure my connection with her because it taught me so much about the Hispanic culture that I was unaware of. There have been many white women that I have developed a relationship with and we share experiences and stories that have challenged our mindset and character.

Over the years, God has challenged me to see the heart of the person and not their skin color. I have learned to have honest conversations that can be tough. It's very challenging to not wear a chip on our shoulder with injustice in the land.

About LaVal

LaVal Ezell is a well-respected Certified Life Coach, Sisterhood Strategist, motivational speaker, and blogger among women. She has personally mentored women of all ages for over 15 years and enjoyed every moment.

It's also her passion and mission to galvanize girls and women into a lifestyle of authentic sisterhood. "Self-Worth inspires Sisterhood" is what she echoes into the hearts of women. LaVal has conducted life-skills programs, workshops, conferences, and special events for girls and women in the Dallas-Fort Worth area and surrounding states. Her passion for healthy friendships among women has birthed a movement called Striving In Sisterhood, which teaches strategies for the levels of friendship and biblical sisterhood. Striving In Sisterhood has developed into a community of women that attend the Striving In Sisterhood Seminars and The Sister Sit & Chat Experience for self-discovery, relationship strategies, maturity in the levels of friendship, accountability, and purpose. The Sister Sit & Chat Journey Experience was created for women to build and bond with other women that also desire healthy friendships. LaVal has traveled to many cities and states for women to experience this movement. She believes that sisterhood creates a bond, loyalty, and love that's rarely enjoyed, yet should be experienced by every woman. Her mission is to teach and inspire all women to seek their worthiness and learn to be a woman that Believes, Receives, and Achieves the Art of Sisterhood.

LaVal has been happily married for 18 years. She and her husband have a blended family with two daughters and a son who are developing leaders. LaVal and her family are members of Anchor Church in McKinney, TX.

Chapter 14
"The Melanin of My Skin"

By Alisha N. Cole

"What has been will be again, what has been done will be done again; there is nothing new under the sun." (Ecclesiastes 1:9 NIV)

Unfortunately, I believe racism and social injustice is a long way from being over. History has taught us that one race always has and always will view themselves as more superior than the other.

Racism and Social injustice can be traced as far back as the biblical days; from the enslavement of the Hebrews, by Pharaoh, to the American Indians, by foreigners that stole their land; from the Blacks of African descent, who were brought from their homeland to a foreign land to be sold as slaves, to human and sex trafficking.

The Prophet Isaiah said, *"Woe to those who make unjust laws, to those who issue oppressive decrees, to deprive the poor of their rights and withhold justice from the oppressed of my people."* (Isaiah 10:1-2a NIV).

Jesus also addressed these issues during his time on earth (Matthew 18:21-35).

Racism or Social Injustice was never a part of God's plan. When we read Genesis 1:26-27, there was not a distinction between race, ethnicity, or gender: *"God created male and female in his likeness and gave them dominion of the fish, of the sea, and over the fowl of the air, and over the cattle, and over all the earth, and over every creeping thing that creepeth upon the earth."* This dominion was never meant to be exploited or misused to lord over another person.

However, as time progresses, we can see how man took that which was good and corrupted it. According to history, slavery initially began in the United States in 1619, when The White Lion ship brought 20 African slaves to the British Colony of Jamestown, VA.

It was not until Abraham Lincoln initiated the Emancipation Proclamation on September 22, 1862, and made it official on January 1, 1863, that our people were deemed free-ish. However, to those in Galveston, TX, it was another two and a half years before they were made free-ish. Even after being freed, people of color have always been victims of racial and social injustice. This ranges from low paying jobs to redlining, police brutality, longer prison sentences than other races who commit the same crime, lack of medical care, and the list goes on and on.

As a small child, I remember my father being referred to as the "N" word, by an older Caucasian man. Hearing that word brought many questions to my young mind. Why was my father called outside of his name? Why didn't he say anything to the man? What was the “N” Word? Am I an “N” Word because my father is one? Why did my father just walk away? It was at that moment I realized there was something different about me, my father, and others that looked like me. I did not know what the word meant, but I knew it was something ugly, something meaningful, and something that was said out of hatred towards my father.

What is it about our melanin skin that causes others to hate it, yet envy it, and yet try to emulate it? From the fullness of our lips to the curviness of our hips. To the fullness of our butts, and even the kinkiness of our hair. Our music, the way we talk, and everything about us are being copied by other races that feel we should be inferior to them.

Now that I am older, I realize that ugly "N" Word was meant to emasculate my father. I also understand why my father never addressed the man for calling him outside of his name. My father grew up in an error where blacks and whites were not allowed to go to school together or even drink from the same water fountain.

Even though my father never addressed the man, I could see the anger and rage in his eyes from the blatant disrespect he had just experienced. Even though he had this negative experience of being called outside of his name, my father taught me never to allow another person's ignorance to cause you to act out of character.

My father and my mother also taught my siblings and me to rise above the shallowness of another person's behavior. Just because they call you outside of your name or treat you less than a person does not mean you have to answer or become the person they have labeled you to be. It is not what they call you; it is how you respond, that depicts as to whether or not you are who they labeled you to be. Always aim high and never low is what our parents taught us.

Even when our family lost our family home due to forged documents by a Caucasian woman, I watched my mother and father handle the injustice of the judicial system with dignity and pride. It never stopped them from moving forward. I questioned what was so special about our family home that another person felt the need to befriend my parents by offering to assist them in their time of need, as a rouse to illegally gain possession of our family home, through a biased judicial system. My parents had proof that the documents were forged; however, it is in my opinion that they were denied justice because of their melanin skin color.

Even though this injustice, my parents never allowed us to see them sweat. They graciously moved out of the home and turned the keys over to someone whom they once called a friend. I could not comprehend what I was seeing as a child. I knew it was wrong, yet I felt safe and secure because my parents kept strong. Watching my parents navigate through the many injustices they experienced throughout my childhood, (from threats of burning a cross in our front yard, to a letter taped to our front door stating "N-word get out of our neighborhood, you're on the wrong side of town"), these experiences equipped me with the strength, wisdom, and knowledge I would need later on in life.

As an adult, I have had my fair share of racism and social injustices. One of many incidents comes to mind. I was about twenty-one years old, working for a family-owned telecommunications company. Like any new employee, I tried to show myself friendly and learn the ropes of the new company.

I will never forget it; it seems like it was just yesterday. I had become quite friendly with one of my colleagues. We would go to lunch together, hang out with each other's families, and significant others; we were the best of friends, so I thought.

On this one particular day, the person who I thought was my friend (a Caucasian woman) made an inappropriate comment towards me, and I brushed it off because I figured they were having a bad day, and they really did not mean what they had just said to me. However, as the day progressed, they continued with the harassment and called me the "N" Word, which struck a particular chord within me because it was a word that I had heard both my father and mother be referred to as, on various occasions throughout my childhood.

I immediately addressed the issue with the person. I tried to address the situation in a cool and calm manner; however, their aggression continued. So, I reported the incident to HR, not knowing the person over HR was their family. After reporting the incident, I went back to work for the day and took the next couple of days off, as recommended by HR. Unbeknown to me, the incident did not stay between myself, HR, and the person involved. News of the incident echoed throughout the company halls.

When I returned to work, I received all kinds of crazy looks. A white male made a donkey/pig noise as I walked by. The place I once loved to work had now become a hostile work environment. With my head held high, I grabbed my things to leave for the day. On my way out the door, the person (a Caucasian woman) who I thought was my friend, was walking down the hallway toward my direction. As I proceeded to get on the elevator, she put her hand in the elevator to keep the doors from closing. As I turned to see what she wanted, she proceeded to spit in my face and call me the "N" word again; I was horrified!

In my mind, I envisioned myself reaching out and touching her as she had never been touched before.

However, before I could respond, a calmness came over me, and I could hear my parents' voices echoing in my head, “Do not allow this one bad moment in time to take you out of character.” As I was gathering the wills about myself to stay calm, which was very hard, by the way, I heard a small still voice say, “Hold your peace.” For me, that was it. I ended up taking the rest of my accumulated sick and vacation days, with thoughts of never returning to that place again.

On the third or fourth day of my vacation, I started receiving phone calls advising me that if I had any personal items at the job, I should come and get them. The company lost its lease and was filing for bankruptcy and moving to another state, under a new name.

At that moment, I felt vindicated and angry at the same time. I felt vindicated because no one else would ever have to deal with the nightmare I dealt with. I also felt angry because of the humiliation I experienced. As a child, I promised myself I would never allow anyone to disrespect me and make me feel less than human.

The experience I gained at that moment was life-changing. It made me realize that racism was just as prevalent then, as it was in my parents’ day and age and their parents’ parents’ day and age. Racism has existed since the beginning of time.

I read earlier this year; I don't remember exactly where I read it. However, the article stated that studies have shown that "African Americans, Latinos, and Asian Americans suffer more job discrimination than that of a less qualified Caucasian male or female in a given year who applies for the same job." Reading that article rang truth throughout my spirit and sparked several questions. How is it that we are living in the 21st Century and we are still dealing with an age-old issue that started with Cain and Abel.

I am reminded of another incident of racism that happened to a friend of mine. She graduated from high school in the summer of '74. She was 18 and ready to take on the world! She needed a car to get back and forth from school and work, so her father helped her by consigning on her first car purchase (a lemon). She was working summers through a job training program that was funded by the government, and she was hopeful about the outlook of her future!

Through the program, she worked at the airport full-time in the summer and part-time during the school year. During the second school year, the program was defunded, and her job at the airport was terminated. She had no job, no money, and a car payment on a car that was not running because it needed a new engine.

In an effort to keep her father's credit healthy and to get her transportation going, she searched diligently for another job, and the process was brutal. It was a long search, and she got discouraged and depressed. Finally, out of desperation, she took a job at a cafeteria located in a corporate building about 10 miles from her home. She got up at 4 o'clock every morning to catch two buses and walk 3 miles from the bus stop to reach the building and clock in by 6 a.m. She was the only black person working there among a group of Latinos who only spoke Spanish but understood English. Consequently, she had no one to talk with during her shift. She was hired at startup, so her initial job entailed performing a lot of industrial work, but her actual role was to maintain the dessert section in the food service area. It was a very demanding and lonely job, but she had major responsibilities to take care of.

After working there for about a month, one particular morning, she took her break as usual, following the breakfast rush. She was tired, and as she walked towards a table to sit and rest, she casually strolled past a table where the owner and a couple of his managers were sitting. No one else was in the cafeteria at the time, and she was walking in a relaxed posture with her hands in her pocket. As she passed their table, the owner looked at her and ordered her to remove her hands from her pocket. "Take your hands out of your pocket!" he said, “You look trifling!" Mind you, this was the second time he had spoken to her. The only other time was on the day of her interview with him.

The look on his face was that of disgust, and she was crushed. She had never heard anyone say anything like that to her before. She came from a proud, hard-working, and supportive family, and they took their responsibilities seriously. She thought to herself, “I’m getting up early in the morning... Monday through Friday...and walking in the dark to catch two buses...and walking 3 miles from the final bus stop...through a secluded area...to get to a job that only gives me a total of 40 minutes for an eight and a half hour shift for breaks... and all he can do is assess the word "trifling" to my rest time?” She replied to him, "I'm on a break." He told her that was fine but walking around with her hands in her pocket was trifling, so "Take them out when you're here." Her ears got hot, and she looked him straight in the eyes and said, "I'll show you trifling, I quit!"

He told her that she could not quit because it was almost lunchtime. She said, "That is not my problem, sir. I will come back to pick up my check on Friday." She turned and walked boldly and briskly to her locker, got her belongings, clocked out, and she 'left the building'! At that moment, she felt relieved and fearless. A week later, a job opened up where her boyfriend’s mother worked, and she was hired there.

What she learned was, while racism involves color and cultural differences, it is really about the union of self-interest and insensitivity. Color and culture merely help to identify the racist thread. That man did not care about her or her needs. He only cared about what he wanted, and he did not care about how he would get it—he saw workers, not people. Her Latino co-workers did not care that as they helped each other get through the day by sharing their stories and thoughts verbally, they were excluding her from the group by only speaking in a language she could not understand. Surely, they spoke enough English for general conversation. How else would they communicate their qualifications to secure their employment?

God gave the 10 Commandments primarily for the purpose of teaching us how to be caring and sensitive towards each other, and personally. When Jesus was asked what the greatest or most important Commandment of all was, He summed it up in 3 principle ideas; love God, love others, and love oneself (Luke 10:27). Love is the key to overcoming racism; patience, giving, kindness, gentleness, caring, sensitivity, and support (1Corinthians 13:4-8).

Neither the cafeteria owner nor the Latino (Spanish only speaking) co-workers needed to know her story to be civil towards her. It should have been a given to be sensitive to her human nature—considering she has feelings also. And that is what racism survives and thrives on—a lack of consideration and sensitivity to how another may feel about our actions or words. Everyone in that cafeteria was making viable contributions to a common goal and common courtesy and sensitivity could have made that assignment a pleasant experience for everyone involved. Racism is a spiritual matter of the heart, and it can only be defeated by a heart matter—love.

Witnessing racism and or social injustice is one thing, but experiencing it is an entirely different beast. At the core of racism is pure hatred, and hatred is learned behavior, in my opinion. However, accounting to May Ling Halim, an associate professor of psychology at California State University of Long Beach, and Sarah Gaither, an assistant professor of psychology and neuroscience at Duke University, racism comes from the underlying psychological and cognitive functions that lead us to see and categorize people by color (cnn.com/health).

When a child is firstborn, they see no color. Everyone looks the same. However, as "early as three months, babies can distinguish faces by color". It is not until a child gets older (3yrs) that he or she is "fully capable of understanding racial categories and even the hierarchies that come from them" (cnn.com/health). As parents, legal guardians, caregivers, etc., it is our responsibility to teach our children good core values while they are young. It is these values that will mold and shape them into the person they will become later on in life.

Sarah Gaither said in an interview with CNN, "I don't think anyone's kid is born racist. Children are born into a world that has systemic racism, and they're born into a culture that harbors racist attitudes and racist ideologies, and those ideologies seep into everything. If someone is harboring certain racist attitudes, it's something that they are learning from their parents, schools, the media, and the culture" (cnn.com/health).

I found Gaither's comment to be true, especially when she said, our culture influences racism. As a black female entrepreneur, I have found myself being overlooked by potential customers because of the ethnicity of my skin. As a black business owner, there is some egregious stigmatism associated with "Black Owned." The sad part is it is not just the other nationalities or races that are hesitant about doing business with a black-owned business; it's also those of my same race. When most people hear black-owned, they immediately think of cheap, poor customer service, poor quality, bad attitude, poor marketing, poor location. All of these negative stigmas are culture driven.

It is amazing how we as a society are influenced by the things we hear, see, and feel from various outlets in life, our parents, educators, pastors, media, friends, frenemies, etc.… We have become a society that judges others based on what was said and not by what we know of them personally.

I remember as a child reading about Black Wall Street in Tulsa, Oklahoma, and how booming and successful the community of Greenwood was. Our people were black and proud. We supported our own. We had our own bank, luxury homes, restaurants, movie theaters, stores, etc. It wasn't until the allegation of attempted rape of a white woman by a black man that things in the community of Greenwood changed. Without hesitation and/or further investigation of the allegation, a mob of armed and angry whites destroyed Greenwood. It is said that roughly 300 people died, hundreds were injured, and roughly nine thousand became homeless.

Peace, justice, and equality is something that each person must pose within themselves to want it for someone else. Without this, our fight for justice and equality for all will continue to be an uphill battle. I am reminded of a song sung by Jackie Deshannon "What the World Needs Now Is Love. It is the only thing that there is just too little of."

Jesus told his disciples in John 13:35, *"By this shall all men know that ye are my disciples if ye have love one to* another. I John 4:20 says, *"If a man says, I love God, and hateth his brother, he is a liar: for he that loveth not his brother whom he hath seen, how can he love God whom he hath not seen?"*

Until genuine love flows from every human heart, from the inside out, we must continue to speak out loud and cry out against institutionalized racism and social injustice from the White House to the Church House to the Judicial system. There are so many racial injustices in our Housing, Education, and Medical Care systems.

Equal pay in Corporate America and Non-Corporate America is also a big issue. According to www.leanin.org, "On average, Black women in the U. S. are paid 21% less than white women. Black women ask for promotions and raise at about the same rates as white women, but they get worse results. The gap is largest for Black women who have bachelor's and advanced degrees."

The only way this battle can be won is if we lay down our bayonets and arrows against one another and stand hand and hand to strategically fight through our voting and our petition to change biased legislative laws that are designed to cage those who the law was never meant to protect.

So, let us rise up and speak out. We must share our truth so that others may learn from our experience and continue to carry the torch for racial equality, social justice, and peace for every man, woman, boy, and girl of all creeds, nationality, origin, race, or gender.

We are all in this together and remember, God desires each of us to be prosperous in every area of our lives; Spiritually, mentally, physically, financially, and socially, but it is up to us as individuals to apply his principles to our daily lives. Without love for our fellow man, we are doomed as a people to continue from generation to generation the same cycles of racism and social injustices until the end of time.

References

CNN.com/health (2020, June 6). Children aren't born racist.

Here's how parents can stop them from becoming racist: https://www.cnn.com/2020/06/06/health/kids-raised-with-bias-wellness/index.html

US Census Bureau.gov (2018). OCCUPATION BY SEX AND MEDIAN EARNINGS IN THE PAST 12 MONTHS

https://data.census.gov/cedsci

About Alisha

Alisha Cole is a native of San Diego, California, and she is the second eldest child of three siblings. Alisha moved to Dallas, Texas in 1989, where she met her husband, Pastor Reginald Cole, in 1996 and united in holy matrimony in November 2006. In Oct 2014, Alisha was ordained as an Associate Pastor.

Not knowing then that her move to Texas was God-ordained, Alisha experienced many of life's hardships, including racism, social injustice, and the death of her unborn child. Overcoming many obstacles of her past, she exemplifies the personification of a true leader. God has anointed her to minister to women of all walks of life.

Alisha has acquired many accomplishments that have molded her to be the Woman of God she is today. In April of 2010, she founded "The Proverbial Women's Ministry," where she teaches and addresses everyday issues of the Christian Woman. Through the ministry of The Proverbial Woman, Alisha teaches biblical principles to women who want to establish themselves as Godly entrepreneurs, wives, mothers, and ministers that God has called to the forefront for such a time as this.

In August 2014, Alisha launched TNT Kingdom Principles & Revelation. In February 2015, she launched The PWM Kingdom Blog Talk Radio Show. In January of 2020, she officially launched a home-based t-shirt and logo business called "Nikki's Logos & Design."

Chapter 15
"He Is King"

By Shameeya K. Johnson

It’s a boy!!!!

After hearing those words, the room got extremely quiet to the point you could hear my tears hit the floor. I was so angry on the inside. For one, I didn't plan on getting pregnant, and I didn't want a boy. Since I was pregnant, I was expecting a girl. At least that's what I thought. It was so much I planned on doing with my little girl, which just showed my level of immaturity, to think I could control my child's gender. I thought how cute it would be for us to dress alike and go to the nail shop together. And as light as her skin tone would have been, she could have it so much easier in this world than a boy ever could.

But it was deeper than that. I wanted my daughter back that I lost a few years prior. I felt I could get my daughter back by having another. Or at least get a taste of what life would have been like with her. So, I was angry because God didn't allow me to have my way again!

It felt like silence lasted forever while sitting in a dark room alone, but in reality, I wasn't alone. Finally, snapping out of it, I could hear my son's father shouting my name, "Shameeya! Are you good? You ready to go?" The white nurse looked at me, …smiling. As I wiped my belly clean and adjusted my clothes, she made a statement that sounded more like a question, "Seems like you were expecting different results…?" “Yes!”, I responded with a slight attitude. As this white nurse rubbed my shoulders, mentioning how her two boys were so much fun and very active, it was at that moment; I knew she was clueless to the fact that we lived in two different worlds.

She couldn't possibly think that my black son would have the same walk through life as her white sons. But all I did was smile and nod as I walked right out of the door and back into my world, to figure out how I was going to make it through life with a black baby boy on the way. I quickly looked at my son’s father for answers, since he has dealt with the reality of being a black man in this country, struggling to survive. How was I going to raise a black boy in the so-called “United” States of America? I remember telling my son’s father to make sure he sticks around to teach our son everything it is to know about our history and to tell him how he made it through his personal experiences.

It was now our job to make sure he understands our history, our current reality, and what it means to build character in a mean world. His father told me that as his mother, it's important for me to connect with my son and teach him how to be kind and loving. “He needs a good relationship with his mother because you’re the first woman he will fall in love with and call on when in need. Most of his time will be spent with his mother," he said. I never thought to look at things that way, but I am forever grateful it was brought to my attention. I was just so used to thinking the worst in every situation. That way, I could be prepared for it when it does happen. But I found myself more depressed, and going through life like that, wasn't healthy for me.

I took a few minutes to deal with my emotions and allow myself to be hurt---and then I had to come out of it. There was absolutely no time to waste, be upset, or feel sorry for myself. It was time to grow up and take accountability for my actions. So, mommy-to-be kicked it up a notch because it was no longer about me. Knowing how strong-willed I am and how badly I wanted to make a change in my life (and others), I became the best mother I could, because there was a job that needed to be done.

During my pregnancy, I made sure I took care of myself, ate healthily, read to my son, and rested very well. Also, I had to take a few more extra precautions to get my son here safely, as well as making sure I survived to see him grow up. For nine straight months, I had to give myself shots in my stomach, which were blood thinners. That put me in a very dark space, almost to the point where I just wanted to give up. God had already taken a child from me, so I was afraid that he would do it again. But he had something else planned for our lives, "I have come too far now to give up" is what I told myself every single day. If taking those shots was going to help me get my son here safely, I was going to do just that. I could not imagine going through life, losing another baby. Mentally, I was a lot stronger than I thought I was.

Sitting in that doctor's office while the nurse demonstrated to me how to give myself shots was an exceedingly difficult time for me. It was so overwhelming to make sure I switched sides when giving myself these shots daily, making sure I cleaned the area first, and most of all, not forgetting. It was so painful, and I hesitated every time, literally having to talk myself through it. Most times, I just sat on the toilet, asking God why…but royalty was developing inside of me.

We made it! I did it! Giving birth to my son was the most amazing experience of my life. At that moment, I just wanted me and his father to be alone with him. No one else! To pray over him, allow him to feel the unconditional love his parents have for him, and just to soak up that life-changing moment. I got a second chance at parenthood. We named him King Shaheem Daughtry, the King of intelligence. A real black power name, huh. 12:34 pm April 27, 2018…Happy Birthday!!!

You would not believe me if I told you there was a time when I did not want my son. Yes! This little boy that God blessed me with. I did not want him at all. Finding out I was pregnant when I wasn't ready, but also finding out the anatomy of my child, hit me differently. I realize all the tough challenges he will have to face, just because of the color of his skin. It scares me half to death!

Life for me as a black woman has never been easy, and now that I am a single black woman with a black son, I have an even bigger fight to fight. Our lives can be very scary and dangerous at times because we just never know what's waiting for us on the other side of that door. I not only have to fight to protect myself; it's about protecting my son now, by all means necessary. Because one thing is for sure---America does not care about my son's life. To them, we are nothing more than wild animals that need to be destroyed. But we know that's not true. We are powerful! And our lives matter too!

King motivates me to become a better me inside and outside. I'm determined to give my son everything he deserves as a black boy that's growing into a black man of Royalty. It's bad enough that King will somewhere in his lifetime face racism, and that's a tough situation you can never really prepare yourself for. So, I need to teach him about our world and teach him to operate out of love despite how hard it may be. At the present time, King is two years old, going on 50. He is such a sweet, loving, innocent boy. He loves the outdoors, loves to be at Granny's house playing cards, and just enjoying life as a young boy with no worries.

This is the stage where people think he is so cute and adorable, which is true. That will quickly change when he gets older because then, the world will see him as a threat, and it kills me on the inside. No matter how old he gets, he will still be my loving, innocent little boy. When I think about King getting older and being able to go places alone or with friends, it sends me into a panic instantly. It shouldn't be this way, but it is. When I think back on all the young black boys that have lost their lives simply because someone felt threatened by their skin color and their presence, it hurts like crazy!

Trayvon Martin, for instance, was a 17-year-old African American from Miami Gardens, Florida, who was fatally shot by George Zimmerman. Trayvon was walking back from the store where he purchased a bag a skittles and an Arizona iced tea. Zimmerman assumed because of the way Trayvon was dressed, that he was up to something bad, and took the law into his own hands. Zimmerman shot Trayvon after being told by police not to follow him, but what really crushed me was hearing Trayvon call out for his mother for help. That's the fear I carry in my heart for my son because it has happened to so many young black boys.

Even if my son were in danger, I would not be comfortable enough to tell him to call the police until I made it there, because they might kill him or harm him. But we can no longer live our lives in fear of any human being.

So, I'm living my best life right now! I wouldn't change it for anything in this world! Yes, I know that's a strong statement to make, but I stand by it. God has given me everything I need and more. I just had to see it for myself. My black son is the best thing that has ever happened to me. King! Powerful, intelligent, smart, courageous, genius… and did I mention a King? Please understand me when I say, my son has saved my life in so many different ways, and he has been my teacher. Now some may mistake my love for him as an obsession, and I've even had crazy people tell me I worship my son because of the way I treat him and speak about him. No! It's an honor to be his mother. I speak words of life into my son because nobody else in this cruel world will do so, and I will continue to speak those words until the day I die.

King continues to grow every day and never ceases to amaze me. He has his whole life in front of him. I can't wait to see all the good my son will do in this world and the obstacles he will overcome. I will be there for him every step of the way, as long as God allows me to do so. And as our journey continues, the story will get better and better. Being able to share my story with the world is nothing but God and growth, but mostly God.

-Words of a black man-

"Coming into this world, especially here in America, and being black in America- it's like a gym. No one here knows

you---or wants to get to know you. Most people here feel better and more powerful than you. And these systems, these machines, everything here, is meant to break you. Literally! Many people will last a few weeks, months, and quit. They will be broken, embarrassed, and tired, but some will walk into it head up and ready to beat the fear and stay with it. Some will see the machines as something that will make them stronger, so they plan and commit themselves to come out on top. They will eventually learn how to respect and control the machine. They will learn to use it to make them stronger.

And for the most part, that's what we have done here. Black men in America are the strongest, most resilient. We have swag and the confidence that comes from knowing we've walked in this gym and didn't cower and didn't run. We walked, we pushed back, we loved, we understood, we invented and learned. We stood our ground and kept our hearts, but America is no gym. It's a much crazier place! But we can come out stronger than anyone else. We just have to put in the work".

King's Father

About Shameeya

Shameeya K. Johnson, a resident of Arlington, Texas, is currently a full-time college student majoring in English/Education, as well as an aspiring author. She is the owner of Jewels Playhouse, which provides tailored childcare services, in memory of her daughter, Jewel Ahmire Brown.

Shameeya has appeared in several stage plays and skits, and many may also know her as Meeya J. She is a talented and aspiring actress who is a natural on the stage. Shameeya has a passion for acting, and she possesses the ability to capture her audience while doing her best to make them smile. She is continually moving towards her dreams and goals while being the proud single mother of a handsome, intelligent little boy by the name King S. Daughtry.

Shameeya enjoys hanging out with her best friends and spending time with her family.

Chapter 16
"Misery Loves Company"

By Alicia Rougeau-Varnado

My first declaration is that I am" Unapologetically Black," no if`s, and's, or but's about it.

When approached to be a participant in this prestigious project, like Moses in the bible, I felt inadequate. No, I do not have any letters behind my name; however, I am a very intelligent and knowledgeable grown black woman that can speak in complete sentences.

Considering the conversation that we're speaking on, immediately brought to mind one of my favorite scriptures, which is Psalm 37: 1-2 (NIV), which reads, "Do not fret because of those who do wrong; for like the grass they will soon wither, like green plants they will soon die away."

Just for clarity, I come from a very rich background. When I use the term "rich," it has nothing to do with money or wealth; however, it has everything to do with my forefathers. You see, I am a descendant of slaves and sharecroppers.

My great paternal grandfather, Dennis Rougeau, was mulatto; therefore, he was often discriminated against because he was too dark for the Caucasian community and was too light for the black community, so he couldn't win for losing.

His wife, Mrs. Bridgette Berry, born in 1863 (who was affectionately known as Mom B's), my great-grandmother, was a descendant of slaves from Africa.

One of the children born out of this union was my grandfather, Melvin Rougeau Sr. (Frank). He worked most of his life picking cotton and operating a John Deere tractor in rice fields in the rural areas of Eunice, Louisiana. Most days, he received little or no pay. That resulted in barely being able to feed his wife and children. Some days he may have received currency, and some days he may have received a chicken or something of the sort.

He eventually met and married my grandmother, Caroline Bellow, who had a "free black." Family history has it that her mother, Mary Hawkins, my great grandmother, and other family members, boarded a ship in Spain and set sail for the free world of Native Americans.

I can speak more on the subject of my paternal relatives as opposed to my maternal relative's heritage, because my maternal grandmother, Ethel Antoine, transitioned to be with the Lord when I was just a little girl. I only have vague memories of her. The one thing that does not escape my memory is that she was a very pretty lady with long wavy black hair.

Now that you know a bit of my ancestor's history, let's fast forward to this Twenty-First Century of slavery, racism, and social injustices in these yet to be "United" States of America.

Serving as the Admissions Counselor/Registrar on our campus was my last job. During my nearly ten-year tenure there, we experienced frequent administrative changes. In the course of many transitions, I once had a Caucasian female administrator that I was to report to daily for approval of various projects. On any given day, she would come to me and question a decision that I made on a particular situation. Parenthetically let me say that I was the only "qualified" person on the campus to perform the assigned duties for my said position. The days that I was not at work, whether it was personal, vacation, or an emergency day off, upon my return, enrollments, and records requests, would fill my inbox via electronic mail or hard copy.

Normally I missed a day here or there once a quarter; however, she was always assured to remind me that I wasn't there the day/days before and would never fail to make a demeaning sly remark, which made me feel harassed.

One weekend evening, after leaving work, I received a phone call from my doctor's office, reminding me of an upcoming appointment that was scheduled for that Monday morning. The following Monday morning, I called the principal's secretary to inform her of my tardiness and why. She had directed me, that if at any point I would be late or absent, to text her personally and inform her of my whereabouts. Well, I did that as well. Undoubtedly that was not enough for her. She set out with the intent to make my work life miserable by any means necessary.

She was made aware that I had made it on campus. Instead of calling me in my office to request my presence in her office, she put out an "all-points bulletin" over the walkie-talkie radio, stating, “If anybody sees Ms. Rougeau, let her know she needs to see me in my office ASAP.”

Upon arriving at her office, she didn't even offer me a seat before she proceeded to "reprimand" me for taking the morning off without advance notice. Mind you, I had plenty of unused vacation and sick leave. She proceeded to “chastise” me, mentioning that due to the high demand for my position, she needed more time to make provisions in my absence. The way she made me feel in that office was indescribable. I felt humiliated, hurt, belittled, and mortified.

Her office door was not closed tight, and she had adults and students waiting outside of her office that clearly heard the manner of which she had spoken to me. The most gut-wrenching thing was, in addition to being so very disrespectful, she is only a year or two older than my, now deceased, son.

When the brief meeting was over, I was visibly shaken. I left her office in tears and informed her that I needed to leave for the day. Upon exiting her office, she hollered out, "Next," showing no remorse at all.

Those of you that are wondering if I elevated this to her superiors, yes, I skipped over the principal and called headquarters to her director's office. I'm not sure if she received a slap on the hand or not; however, I doubt it because, in my opinion, that's the nature of the business, they tend to reward bad behavior. I witnessed that district being sailed on three ships, “friendship," “kinship," and “courtship.”

My husband and I just so happened to work on the same campus. Actually, we met and married while working there. He also has stories of racial injustices. In one of his stories, there was a white Colonel from Boston, Massachusetts, that was intimidated by my husband from the first day he met him. That Colonel intended to make my husband’s workday miserable with every fiber of his being.

My husband had been on the campus for years before this particular Colonel's arrival. The students loved my husband, who was known affectionately as "Sgt. V". He was much more than a JROTC instructor to them. He was a life coach, mentor, father/Pa-Pa figure. Most days he bought some of them lunch, gave them rides to and from football games when they had to post the colors, and even took one of them to college out of town because the baby didn't have any other way to get there.

On the morning after President Barack Obama won the presidential election, the Colonel walks into the JROTC office and throws the newspaper on his desk and says, "Oh, I guess y'all (African Americans) won last night." Sgt.V's response was, "No, Sir, we all won," meaning the American people. My husband said it was a racial remark and made him feel like it was a slap in the face to all Black people like he was only going to be African Americans' President and not every races' President.

In preparation for this project, I asked my parents, who actually lived through the "Jim and Jane Crow" segregation, to share a memory or two with me so that I can share with you. My mother, Bernadine Rougeau, expressed that she didn't have nearly as many war stories as my dad; however, she did manage to give me one pretty good example of racism.

She was working back in the early '60s at a nightclub in Eunice. She said that she would go in the late morning or early afternoon to clean from the night before, getting ready for the upcoming day. This particular day, my dad and a friend of the family decided, instead of just dropping her off at work, they would stay in the building and wait for her to complete her tasks. Well, when the white owner realized they weren't leaving, he approached my mom. He told her that if they were to wait on her, they would have to go to the back because if some of his white customers were to come in and see them sitting in the front, that wouldn't be good for his business. My mother said it was a humiliating and racist statement. She said she told him, "Well I'll tell you what, if your white customers can't see them sitting in the front of this building, then this negro don't need to be working in the background cleaning up behind them." She said she dropped that broom never to pick it up again and told him, "You can have this J.O.B."

When interviewing my dad, he shared a story with me that I was completely blown away to hear. He was telling me about him and his younger brother, about a year and a half younger than him, having to go to work with my grandfather at a very early age. He recalled that one day my grandfather's white "boss" said that he wasn't separating the cotton quick enough, so he cracked a whip across his back approximately four or five times.

My dad didn't realize that, as he's telling me this story, tears are falling down my face. I questioned his statement by asking, "So, you are telling me that he cracked a whip on Dad's (that's what we called him) back?" His answer again was "yes." It's still hard to even write about this because I'm saddened that this happened to such a loving, hard-working, gifted, and talented man. Imagine witnessing your loved one getting slashed with a whip. How would that make you feel? My dad told me that it made him feel very angry. He said that he made a promise to himself that when he grew up, he was going to kill that man; however, the Lord said: "Vengeance is mine." By the time my dad reached adulthood, the man was dead.

The silver lining in these horror stories is that the Lord promises to prepare a table for us in the presence of our enemies. He will anoint our heads with oil, and our cup will overflow. (Psalm 23:5)

He promised to make our enemies our footstool.

"When justice is done, it brings joy to the righteous, but terror to the evildoers." (Proverbs 21:15)

In December of 2015, my husband retired from his job, and I resigned from mine. We are now our own bosses and own a catering business. The Lord provides all of our needs and grants our wants. We no longer have to deal with, or answer to, racist "bosses."

My parents are also retired. My dad has retired thrice. God has blessed him to survive three strokes, and his cancer has gone into remission twice.

The Lord has blessed my mother's breast cancer to go into remission, and she's doing well with her chemotherapy treatments.

In closing, I would like to encourage you not to let these social injustices make you a bitter person. Instead, let them make you a better person. You had to experience your wrongdoings for a purpose---on purpose. I would like to leave you a couple of scriptures that may be uplifting to you:

Galatians 6:9 *"Be not weary in your well-doing, for in due season we shall reap if we faint not."*

In part, Matthew 25:23 says, *"...you've been faithful over a few things, so I'll make you a ruler over many."*

I am humbled for the opportunity to share just a smidgen of some of our life's experiences, and I hope they will bless someone.

About Alicia

Alicia Rougeau-Varnado's humble beginnings started in the rural town of Eunice, Louisiana. In her early childhood, she enjoyed the simple small-town experience of Eunice with her siblings and loving parents. However, as with most small towns in America during the 1960s, there were two sides of town. Alicia was too young to see anything but a happy childhood. She was a typical child attending elementary and some middle school in Eunice.

With the hope of providing a better life for their children, her parents moved to Texas in 1968. Alicia finished middle school at Forest Oak Middle School and then attended O.D. Wyatt High School. After high school, Alicia graduated from the International Aviation and Travel Academy, attended Kaplan University, and then Tarrant County College Applied Science Program, majoring in Culinary Arts. Alicia enjoyed a full career until retirement in 2015. Her career included former employers such as American Airlines, Xerox Capital Services/General Electric, and the Fort Worth Independent School District.

The city of Fort Worth provided a landscape that fostered growth and opportunities for Alicia. Her experiences growingup in Fort Worth were many. Some experiences were good, and others were not so good. Alicia candidly shares her experiences with racism and the impact it made on her life.

Today Alicia is a successful Caterer and Private Chef. She resides in Grand Prairie, Texas, with her husband, SFC Roosevelt Varnardo Jr, and their grandchildren Caleb and Candyce.

Chapter 17
"Injustice in a Modern World"

By Lisa Tarpley Tucker

When I think of the injustice of women, it almost turns my stomach. Just to know there is an individual or a group of individuals that have targeted a person based on their skin color or gender makes my blood boil. I thought about my mother, Varnell Barnes Tarpley, born right after the Great Depression, and having to grow up during a time that was so full of racism. I'm reminded of a story she shared with me about being the first black female elevator operator at Woolworth Department Store in downtown Fort Worth, Texas.

They hired her because she didn't look black. Her skin tone was high yellow. She was often asked if she was white or of mixed skin. She often shared how some of the white people treated her because they knew she was black. The words my mother hated the most were "girl" and "Nigger". She said her response to their comments would be, "yes sir" or "yes ma'am."

I've often said to myself, "Lord, I thank you for not letting me grow up in that day and time." But, yet to have my fair share of racism, and my children to experience the same thing. To say that it has gotten better seems to be an understatement.

My mother was a woman of many firsts in her lifetime. She was one of the first black cashiers at Piggly Wiggly. I know some will not know this store because it had closed by the time I was around seven or eight years old. Mother would share when she came home, of how she was so upset because they could not eat lunch with the whites. Also, some of the customers would put the money on the counter because they did not want to touch her hand. But…they didn't mind her bagging their groceries. So much double standard, and yet to this day, it is the same.

I'm reminded of a story my father shared about my mother not being able to ride in the truck with him. You see, my father drove 18 wheelers for a living when they first met. She was so excited to go on long hauls with him. My father's route was the down south areas where racism was at a high. When they would stop to get fuel or food, he would tell my mother to keep her head down and stay close to him. My mother was always very rambunctious, doing things her way. My dad said, "We had to go to the back to order our food." My mother would say, "No, I don't. I can go to the front." My dad said he knew that was the first and only trip with him because she was going to get them hung. Yes, I said, "Hung. 'This was the time and area of "lynching Negros". Needless to say, she never made a trip again with my father unless he was going north. How divided is that? When one part of the country has suffered major racism and discrimination, and the other part of our country hasn't seen the injustice as much.

I remembered when I chose to move my family out of the city of Fort Worth to Grand Prairie, to give my children a better life and education. My major thing was, I didn't want my children to experience someone calling them the "N" word. Well, the subdivision we moved into was very new, and in the school they attended, there were only two black children in the class. One day, coming home from school, my oldest child had her first experience with a little boy calling her the "N" word. Because it was just her, her sister, and another little girl walking with a group of white kids, the white boy felt like calling her that. Before she could say something, a white girl stood up to him, and the other white kids began to talk about him. I asked her how it made her feel. She said, “Mom, he is the stupid one. I told him, ‘You don’t know what the word means.” I told him that word could be any person, even his mother. I, as a parent, I was so

upset because I could have left my children in the area of our old home to ensure that this would not happen. But I talked to my children to let them know that there are, and will be, ignorant people in this world.

Well, needless to say, by the time they were in middle school, the demographics and social economics of our neighbors had changed in Grand Prairie. But what I believe more than anything is, racism is taught. Children don’t think of hating one another because they look different. An adult has taught them that the person with darker skin is beneath them and to treat them differently.

When I reflect as a child growing up in a black community, being bused to a white community was scary. Seeing other children that did not look like me. My first encounter was in the third grade. A white kid called me a fat black nigger. What was so hurtful was that I thought we were friends because we played together. I couldn’t wait to get home to tell my mother. I cried! I was so hurt because other children were laughing. I hated the feeling of knowing I was being judged by my skin, and even my weight. It didn’t make me hate her, what it did was made me work hard so they would look at my achievements instead of my skin color or size.

From that one incident, I have been dealing with life the same way. Here it is, I’m 55 years old, and I see it so much from white women or men, calling me “girl.” I don’t like it, and I often wonder when do I become a woman or lady to them?

But I have to remind myself that they are ignorant people. In order for this to ever change, it will have to be God. There is so much hatred in this world from the past to the present. I often wondered how the discriminating person would feel if it were turned on them. You would think, as a nation, we would be so past this, but as long as there are people who are yet teaching hatred, it will always be here. This is why we, as a people, must teach. We must not just look at color but educate our children on the importance of knowing who they are and how others have fought for them to achieve great things.

This is what I call injustice in a modern world.

About Lisa

Apostle Lisa Tarpley Tucker is an International Conference Speaker, Author, Entrepreneur, and Preacher. She is armed with a word of Destiny for the Nations, and with an accurate and authentic apostolic anointing. Apostle Lisa Tucker is often called upon to speak a life-changing word to God's people.

Her passion is to see people saved, healed, healthy, prosperous, delivered, and whole, which is demonstrated by her dedication and excellence in ministry. Many have received healing and deliverance, with signs and miracles following. People from all walks of life have been delivered from drugs, oppression, and depression, as well as demonic spirits.

With audacious faith, this mother, grandmother, and wife is also the Senior Pastor of Community First Worship Center, a non-traditional church with a cutting-edge anointing and a multi-cultural mission. The core of Apostle Tucker's mission is to reach the lost with the Gospel through love, prayers, and support.

Apostle Tucker is the author of Long Road to Recovery and Long Road to Recovery Workbook and has been on several radio shows, including her own "Pastors Anonymous." She has taken the Gospel to several states, South Africa, and on the water through cruises. Apostle is affectionately known as "The Preacher Lady" and committed to spreading the love of Christ wherever ministry may take her.

Apostle Tucker loves to read, write, teach, and create. She has creative designs, including her own clothing line. She is also the founder of LLT Ministries.

Chapter 18
"Just Because You Are Invited Doesn't Mean You're Accepted"

By Shannon Adams

The reason I decided to share my story is that the time has come for all racial injustice to be exposed. No racial injustice experience is too small or too big. When I was presented with this opportunity to share, I felt I didn't have any significant experience. But then, as I started reflecting over my life, I quickly realized there were many situations that I had suppressed that started flooding my thoughts.

One incident, in particular, came flooding back to my thoughts. But, first, allow me to set the stage. Have you ever had a dream and wrote the goal of that dream down, then worked hard to achieve that goal? And then that amazing day actually came, and what once was a dream, now became a goal realized. You find yourself being offered an opportunity of a lifetime. Yes, I bet you can imagine my level of excitement when that very thing happened to me.

Now let me fill you in on that monumental opportunity that would have the potential of leading me to my dream and goal. This little southern Black American girl grew up in the inner city with big dreams of going to college and one day becoming a fashion buyer. I would have never imagined where I came from in a million years. I would have an opportunity or even a high probability of what presented itself in 1993.

After graduating from college, I was offered an internship with one of the most luxurious retailers in the country. You can't even conceive my excitement. All I could envision was that it is happening; everything I had worked towards was becoming a reality. Now with my foot in the door, all that was left for me to do was to exceed everyone's expectations so that I would be able to remain at what I felt was my dream job. And so, it happened. I was hired full time. Due to my superior service and work ethic, the general manager submitted me for the store's Prestigious Buyers' Program. I had heard of this program while in college and its difficulty to get in the program. Here again, I was elated that what had been a dream for so long was unfolding as a tangible opportunity… I mean, like, I could almost taste it.

But then as time draws nearer for the interviewing process, I become aware that my store adds another prospect for the program. Since we were acquaintances and coworkers, we were very happy for each other being considered for the renowned program. Although realizing we would be among thousands of applicants. After a few trips out of town, experiencing limousine rides, 5-star luxury hotel stays, and the series of grueling interviews, we were both chosen of the final eight. Following this cut, we would return to work together to finalize our internship stint.

Since we had been working very closely within the store, it was very clear to both of us what our strengths and weaknesses were. I have to add here that I have always known I must work ten times harder than my Caucasian contemporaries. This became evident in grade school thru high school, as my mom transported me clear across town to a predominantly white school. I was often envied of being sometimes the only Black American in the classroom. This had become my norm, and by no means did this threaten my character or ability to succeed. At 25 years of age, being the only Black American among the final eight applicants had become a routine setting.

After a few months, it was time for the final interviewing process, which would mean the last of my complimentary Red Carpet indulgences. I made sure I enjoyed every moment and was prepped and equipped to have an outstanding interview. And it was exactly that; the meeting was outstanding. I returned to my store location, feeling really good about the interview. News had even already traveled back to my general manager.

Many weeks later, I arrived at work, was called into a meeting in our executive office, and there sits my General Manager and Human Resources manager. My heart starts racing, and I'm like, "This is it, the moment I've dreamed about and intentionally worked so hard for is about to happen." They start speaking, and I realize they are telling me that out of the eight applicants, two were chosen, and I wasn't one of the two.

You could only imagine the questions I had while dealing with the feeling in my gut. I was hurt and extremely disappointed. I was trying not to express my true emotion at that present time. But because of my stellar performance, I was offered an introductory management position. Although I know that was not the outcome I had hoped for, I was grateful. But then what happens next would be the first encounter of admittance of unfairness and somewhat the appearance of prejudice, presented to me from a colleague. By now, I'm sure you may be wondering about my coworker, who also was an applicant. She comes to me hours later and offers congratulations, and I'm stunned. I asked her, "For what?" She replies, "On getting into the Buyer's Program." I'm perplexed and tell her I didn't get the position. What happens next was totally shocking to me. She looks at me with tears in her eyes and says, "I'm so sorry, I don't understand how I was chosen, and you weren't."

It was at this very moment; I realized that all my years of making sure I worked ten times harder than my Caucasian colleagues was still not enough. I fell into a deep state of pity. Although, in comparison to what's happening today, this may or may not have been a blatant racial injustice. But it is subtle incidents and life experiences as these that mount up and are a regular constant that shouldn't be!!!

On that day, I'm sure my colleague had no idea she did me a favor. By the impact of this occurrence, I became stronger and more confident and very aware of how this world will most likely always operate, which is very unfortunate. Now that I am a mother of 3 beautiful, intelligent, independent thinking young women, it is my responsibility to have a dialogue with them concerning race relations. Those conversations are a staple in my home. I encourage them to have a voice for what's right and to seek understanding. I am honored to be a part of this compilation of stories because I truly believe thru our stories are mountains of hope.

About Shannon

More than just a wife, mother, entrepreneur, top sales producer in retail, fitness enthusiast, and coaching facilitator, Shannon Adams is an inspiration and motivation to many. It is her earlier challenges in life that grounded and molded her to become the woman she is today. Shannon took life's seemingly difficult situations and carved out her place in this world. She lives passionately and with no regrets.

Growing up in the inner city, namely the impoverished Trinity Gardens area, Shannon's mother insisted on a better life for her daughter. Shannon's mother led by example, and when Shannon was in third grade, she took part in a program called Minority to Majority. This program had Shannon bused from the inner-city school to the elite River

Oaks Elementary. Not only was it a different school, a different side of town, different classmates, different educators, but it also evoked a different mindset. This power move on behalf of Shannon's mother changed the trajectory of Shannon's life. The seed has been planted. Thus, Shannon builds momentum and goes on to create a lot of firsts, accomplish many goals, and, more importantly, she learns to love and validate herself. She learns that she is smart and gifted and beautiful and that she has something to offer this world.

So, in life, there is always the road not taken, and no matter what, Shannon has proven time and time again that with faith, hard work, grit, and tenacity, anything is possible. Her future certainly doesn't look like her past because she knows that in life, we are constantly evolving.

With a degree in Fashion Merchandising and Design, it would only make sense for Shannon to become one of the top producers in her 25 tenure at a leading luxury retailer.

Shannon also believes in paying it forward. All of the programs she has created, co-created, or worked with, such as the Texas Youth Ministry Camp, Adams Alliances, SMILE Coaching Program, AcaSoul Explosion, Cornel Angel Award along with other visionary and philanthropic work, is proof of her relentless dedication to making this world a better place.

One of Shannon's greatest accomplishments to date is finding Christ in 1993. She attributes her 23-year marriage to Minister of Music, Steve Adams, and the joy she finds in motherhood, to her three precious daughters, as amongst her greatest successes.

Shannon is a true testament to what can happen when we each decide that we can have an abundant life. Even when life was sometimes difficult and unfair, Shannon rose above her circumstances triumphantly. She proves that no matter what, even against insurmountable odds, her spiritual foundation continues to sustain her, catapulting her to places she never thought possible.

FB https://www.facebook.com/shannondeniseadams

IG shannonadams_poundsaway

Website http://www.ShannonDeniseAdams.com

Chapter 19
"Shush! Unspoken Pain"

By Dr. Sandra Reyna Stanley

My first memory of racism in Fort Worth, Texas, where I grew up, and that I can remember as a child was in the 1960s. My mother, Juanita Stanley, would take us downtown to shop on Saturdays at Leonard Brothers Department Store, which was the first store downtown to desegregate. After the Civil Rights Acts of 1964, the maintenance crew was assigned to remove the "White" and "Colored" signs on the restrooms and drinking fountains, along with them instructing the management staff of the previously white-only segregated cafeteria, to now serve blacks. My mother often shopped at Leonard Brothers, purchasing me and my brother William's annual school clothes, as did many other local black families also do their shopping. There was a large profit made for the store from the black community, which made it a great strategic move for the Leonard Brothers. The removal of the signs was a big deal, and my mother wanted to assure that we could be a part of history and acknowledge this important moment. The greatest impact for me as a child was seeing the imprint of the "White Only" and "Black Only" signs that would still be visible for years even after they were removed.

My second memory was growing up in a neighborhood church. My mother was a widow, and she attempted to give my brother and me the best she could by having us attend church, participate in Sunday School, and Vacation Bible School. William and I are thirteen months apart, dark skin, and could pass for twins, even now. We were at the church when the doors opened, and when my mother was sick, we would have to walk about a half a mile from home to get to the church. She tried to get us a ride on the church van, where often I would overhear certain adults in the church, refer to us as little monkeys and make comments on our blackness. So yes, racism exists even in the church. Because of the shade and darkness of our skin, it resulted in my brother and I not being picked up by the church van. I truly feel we were treated differently--- less than. As soon as I was allowed to have a choice of where to worship, I left that church to attend the Catholic Church where we attended school.

One of my many adult accounts of racism was, as a community leader overseeing the nonprofit Opening Doors For Women In Need (ODWIN) for over seventeen years. There had been some complaints that some young adults were terrorizing the neighborhood with paintball guns and shooting senior citizens walking in the neighborhood. Also, they were shooting at our office building, leaving paint colors (bright yellow, green, orange) defacing the property. We tried so hard to maintain a beautiful outside, with the help of community service volunteers. These volunteers are vital in assisting with maintaining daily tasks, picking up trash, sorting donations, and other tasks. A beautiful young white lady, one of our volunteers, was outside and happened to see the guys as they tagged our building with the paint gun. She was able to get the license plate number, a description of the car, and an eyewitness, an older white homeless gentleman that was not from this neighborhood. My staff immediately called the police. It was an opportunity to catch them while they were still in the area terrorizing helpless senior citizens. It took four phone calls and a direct call from myself complaining to the 911 operator before we finally got someone to respond to the call.

The officer that responded was a young, tall, white officer. The staff and I began to give him all the information we knew and about the eyewitness. I suggested to the officer that he bring the eyewitness inside of my building instead of standing outside, in order to protect the witness and prevent the possibility of retaliation toward him for talking to the police. I expressed that harm could come to him because he was not from the neighborhood and was talking to the police. The officer became very angry toward me, stating to me that he didn't need me telling him how to do his job. After going outside and talking to the guys that were hanging out, the officer went over to the white girl (my volunteer) as she was scrubbing the paint off the building and began to inform her of the status of his investigation. He stated to the young white girl that he was not going to deal with "her" (meaning me) today because we didn't see eye to eye. Her response to his comment was, "No, please, she is in charge, you need to tell her this information". Of course, that made her very uncomfortable, so she hurried to open the door, so I could hear what the Officer was saying, as I was sitting by the door.

She became very upset once it was obvious that the Officer would not even acknowledge my authority as the person he needed to be speaking with. I found it necessary to inform the Officer, "I'm the director and founder of this program, and the overseer of this building. I am who called in the complaint. Any information that you have to share is to be shared with me. So why are you communicating with my volunteer who is doing community service?" I realized what was obvious by then. My volunteer is white. I asked for his badge number and told him I was filing a complaint, but I was sure to apologize for the suggestion that he speak to the witness inside the building rather than on the streets for his protection if that offended him.

I called and made a report to my city councilman, who called a police supervisor to share my concerns about the interaction between the Officer and myself. The result, a week later, after 9 pm. I received a call from his supervisor, who was white, with no empathy, stating that the officer didn't do anything wrong, and he would not make him apologize. I've lived and operated this nonprofit in this community for seventeen years. It would be nice if the officers took time to get to know who operates the business, and not assume that the only white person is the one to respond too.

Most of my life, I have ignored, or I remained silent in my treatment or mistreatment related to racism. It is my prayer that as we have the opportunity to share these experiences, that others will listen and become educated on racism and begin to respect others. The greatest gift is love. Let's practice it.

About Dr. Sandra

During Sandra Stanley's volunteer service of five years in the prison ministry at The Potters House of Dallas and serving with the only faith-based program in Texas, LCP Program of Federal Prison; Ms. Stanley saw a flawed system within the transitional process of men and women from incarceration. This greatly impacted her and moved her to action to become a real proponent of positive change. It was then the idea of Opening Doors for Women In Need began to form.

Sandra Stanley, CEO of Opening Doors for Women in Need (ODWIN), founded the organization in 2003. Well recognized for its reentry program, it is Ms. Stanley's mission to be an active component in reducing the recidivism rate. There are real barriers men and women face when reentering society after being incarcerated; a lack of support systems, having no place to live, and lack of employment history or education. Far too often, this results in men and women returning to the prison system. Ms. Stanley has made it her goal, through ODWIN, to Change A Life! The Nehemiah Project provides unique advantages for those reentering society by providing a structural system through a transitional housing program for women, along with job readiness. On the job training opportunities for men and women allows them to train in retail sales, small business management, and office administration.

Dr. Stanley completed a dual degree program, earning her Master's and Doctorate in August of 2019 at Integrity Seminary, and she is actively helping to bring positive change for men, women, and families.

Accreditations/Education/Areas of Service:
Recognized and Honored by Great Women of Texas
The FTW Business Press
The City of Fort Worth 2007 Outstanding Women of Fort Worth
Fort Worth Metro Black Chamber of Commerce Women's Division 2013 Eagle Award
Certified Respiratory TCC

Practicing Technician 20yrs. Tarrant County Hospital District
B.S. Allied Health Education UT Southwestern Medical Center, Dallas, TX
Areas Served:
Board Member of The American Lung Association
Director of Minority Outreach North Texas Region American Lung Association
President and Vice President Continuity of Care
Chairman NESEAM Senior at Home program
Exec. Planning Committee Senior Day at the Zoo, Senior Health & amp; Wellness Fair
Team Leader Alzheimer's Memory Walk
Walk Chair for The Walk to Fight Asthma
Honored by Great Women of Texas
Recognition of Fort Worth Business Press
Educational Programs & Groups Implemented and Established
The Better Breathing Club JPS Hospital
National Association of Director of Nurses NADON Kindred Hospital

Chapter 20
"Who Do You Think You Are?"

By Dieadrea S. Mullen

About 20 years ago, not realizing back then that this racial injustice would somehow be relevant today. I can say I had a "the voice" experience. You know, like on the voice, how the judges only hear your voice, but they don't know what you look like until they hit the buzzer and turn their chair around. To their surprise, they had no idea who the person was behind the voice they just heard.

I was at a place in my life, looking to remain in the same career path or make a change as a single Mom providing for my two daughters. I was in between jobs frequently, just trying to survive. Then for this racial injustice to occur, it made me feel like I was unjustly discriminated against.

As I was job searching, I came across a job for a front desk office assistant with experience in all the office products, customer service, and secretarial duties. I submitted my resume for the job even though I knew it was not close enough to my home and daycare to pick up my children. At this point, I knew I needed a job and would figure out the rest later.

The company reached out via email to schedule a telephone interview with me. I was so excited because I knew I had the skills and was willing to work. The phone interview took place a few days later. Upon completion of the interview, the person conducting the interview scheduled me to come in for testing and another interview.

Feeling very optimistic, I was confident that I would go in, rock these tests, and make a great impression. I could be professional and get the job done. As I had been working with a temporary agency for years and other work-related experience in the area they were hiring for.

I got in my car and drove over 20 miles from my residence to this beautiful high-rise building with luxurious floors and furniture. To my surprise, when I walked in, there were several other ladies of all races waiting as well. The front desk receptionist greeted me and asked me if I was there for an interview. I replied, "Yes." She then asked me to sign in on a clipboard that was on her desk. I then walked confidently to have a seat amongst everyone else. While waiting, I noticed there were a few Caucasian ladies that were coming out of this big door to the right of the receptionist's desk. They continued one after the other, in maybe twenty minutes intervals. They would be laughing and smiling while shaking hands with a Caucasian lady that was seeing them out the exit door. I guessed it was the person conducting the interviews.

After a while, a well-dressed Caucasian lady comes to the receptionist's desk and picks up the clipboard that I was signed in on. She began conversing with the receptionist then walked away. The number of candidates in the room started to dwindle as people were being called back. My mind was occupied with this negative thought of "Why is it taking so long if my phone interview went well, and they wanted me to come in." Finally, she came back, looked on the clipboard, and attempted to say my name. She pronounced it so badly.

I proceeded to walk to the front desk, and she was looking around as if she was still waiting for someone. She finally acknowledged me, "Oh, is your name, Dieadrea Mullen?" I responded in a non-defensive manner, "Yes, my name is Dieadrea Mullen." The look on her face was total disbelief as if she was disappointed that I was not who she expected. She looked to be thinking, "You are here now. I must bring you back. I can't tell you no in front of everybody." We proceeded through the same door that I noticed the other ladies leaving out of earlier.

I was astonished! I concluded that this Caucasian lady thought that I was Caucasian because of my diction and professionalism during the phone interview.

Now that I had such an unpleasant feeling, there was no way she could say anything that would make me feel she was not discriminatory due to my skin color. This uneasy feeling made it very hard for me to concentrate on taking the skills test. My palms were sweaty, and I was a little nervous because I was still in disbelief at her response. Other ladies were also testing in the same area. Now in my mind, I thought I would be in the room alone testing. As difficult as it was, I persevered and finished.

My test results were in the 99% percentile, which was excellent. By now, I was one of two ladies left to interview. The anticipation as I waited was unnerving because I had not seen the lady that was surprised by who I was. Would she be the one to interview me? Because I felt like she already didn't like me or was prejudiced towards me. Would my skills outdo her impression of me? Should I just change the way I talk to get the job or just be myself? I struggled with the question, "Should I address the issue, or shouldn't I?" since I was the one needing the job. I was even thinking about the ladies before me that came out the door by the receptionist's desk laughing and leaving with handshakes. I wondered if they had already been offered the job. Was I just being taken through the process to help meet their company's minority quota? I had doubts and fears going through my mind, as I was thinking about my children, as a single Mom having to provide for them.

After the skills test, they called me back through another door in the testing area for the interview. I was relieved that it was not the Caucasian lady that seemed biased, but someone else. That interview went well. She stated that my qualifications and skill set test placed me along with another candidate, and they would get back with me in a few days. About a week later, I received the notorious email that most companies send out. It stated, "Another candidate was chosen for the position, and we will keep your resume on file for future reference."

This experience took an emotional toll on me that day. To be confident in my ability to work hard and professionally but met with racial discrimination because of my skin tone and my voice. Being singled out in a room full of Caucasian, Hispanic, and African American women felt devastating. Then to be turned down for the job.

I learned that day; it does not matter how good you are. People will judge you based on your looks because your voice doesn't match the look expected. A manifestation of racial bias occurred based on my articulation alone. How could my articulation alone cause someone to presume that I was of another ethnicity than my race? I had no idea because of the way that I conversed with others, that it would cause someone to presume I was of another ethnicity. Having a professional voice and using correct grammar and tone when having conversations with others, this I had learned early on in my life. My whole purpose is always to reflect that. That day I learned not to shy away from who you are and that you must ignore the ignorance. Experience and professionalism have no color, and no one should be treated indifferently.

Every job that I accepted, whether it was a temporary assignment or permanent, I still put in all that I had to glorify God. My continued hard work and dedication landed me on a job as a temporary worker with a company. Within three months, they made me a team lead, and I began to climb up the corporate ladder to Functional Lead in Management with my team of employees. Now I was able to interview and hire employees. I never discriminated against anyone, as I had been a victim and did not want to victimize anyone else.

My Dad's Story

Being a dedicated and consistent worker, he wanted to advance his career by furthering his education. He had been working on his job and had to go through an HR process to have paperwork filled out to attend a community college.

He had already moved up in the ranks on the job because of his hard work. There was a higher position that he applied for and had to interview with a Caucasian supervisor. He had other employees working under him that he helped supervise. All the experience and years of service were not good enough, as he was turned down for the position. He found out later they wanted to bring someone in they knew personally. I remember him talking about how well the interview went, but he felt as though they did not want him in that position. If he had gotten the position, it would have put him closer to his desire to advance. He was upset that he would be training the new person, as she did not have the experience needed for the job. They also hired a new guy to work under my Dad's supervision, and he was Caucasian as well. This person decided he would go back and report everything they worked on to the new Supervisor. One day the new employee failed to complete a task my Dad had left for him to do, and my Dad had to write him up.

The gentleman lied and said that he completed the work and that my Dad did not like him. My Dad had to defend himself against a new employee that he was over. The new supervisor called them both into the office and questioned my Dad more extensively as if it was his fault. The supervisor asked these questions in front of the employee that was under my dad's supervision. But my Dad had logs and checklists to show what he had assigned and what was not completed. She was surprised that he had details of the work they had been working on. Instead of her terminating the employee due to the level of the infraction, she gave the employee a warning.

He continued training her as well as the new employee, as he still had a goal to reach. She assumed, as a Caucasian, that his ability to get the job done was less than efficient because of the color of his skin. Instead of my Dad allowing someone to belittle and discriminate against him, it pushed him further. It gave my Dad more drive to further his education, which prompted him to complete the paperwork for Community College. This paperwork had to be signed by the supervisor before it went to HR. She told him, "I don't see why you are filling this out. You won't get in or move to any other positions." My dad said he knew that day without a doubt; it was racism right in his face. She held out for weeks to complete his paperwork. He even went to someone else higher in authority. After several weeks of going back and forth with management, he was able to get someone to sign off on the paperwork.

Then, she changed his hours after he had scheduled his hours to attend Community College. I remember him telling me how upset it made him, but he refused to quit. My Dad was a hard worker for his family, as well as going to Bible college at the same time. This put him in an unpleasantly difficult situation. We had to adjust as a family to ensure that he was able to attend both college and work.

Eventually, my Dad completed his college hours and graduated. He ended up moving into another area away from the supervisor. He had his own office and more employees were reporting to him. My Dad demonstrated to me that you can never let anyone hold you back from moving forward with anything you desire to better yourself.

Being committed, professional, positive, and assured of who you are as a minority will cause some intimidation to others, but don't diminish who you are. Be bold, be brave, stand in who you are.

Hopefully, my stories will intentionally push you to be you no matter what the situation, circumstance, prejudice, or social injustice. So, when someone asks, "Who do you think you are?" you will know within yourself who you are, no matter the color of your skin.

About Dieadrea

Dieadrea Shanta Mullen was born in Hattiesburg, Mississippi, and is the 3rd of 4 children to Edward & Lillie Mullen. Dieadrea says she was raised in the nurture and admonition of the Lord. Dieadrea always stayed in the kitchen to observe her mother cooking. That's when she wasn't busy fighting her brother over Tonka toy trucks and climbing trees.

Dieadrea is a loving, caring mother who has four beautiful daughters, as well as (6) grandchildren who affectionally call her "Nana" and resides in Dallas, Texas. She is currently a Teacher's Aide with her local School District. She started her business "As Unto Him Services," providing resumes, typing, and administrative services in 2001. Dieadrea firmly believes that only what she does for Christ will last. Dieadrea likes to encourage others with a familiar scripture, Proverbs 3:5-7.

During her younger years, she enjoyed dancing and telling jokes. Her friends described her as 'full of wit, humor, sweet and loving."

Dieadrea was a volunteer while serving at Dayspring Christian Center and served on the Dayspring Community Restoration Agency in DeSoto, Texas. Dieadrea is a former member of B.A.D.D. Dance Ministry at her former church Agape Christian Fellowship, Arlington, Texas. She loves to praise and worship God. She has choreographed praise dances and written biblical plays.

Dieadrea was blessed to complete the Daughters of Zion Leadership Mentoring Program in 2004, founded by Thelma Wells.

Dieadrea has been a long time and faithful member of Overflowing Life Ministries, Pastors Anthony and Felecia Wesley, located in DeSoto TX, where she serves in many roles.

Chapter 21
"Director by Default"

By Deborah Williford Simpson

It is 1986; I am 30 years old, married, and the mother of a one-year-old son. It's 4:00 am, and I am no longer able to sleep. I am sitting thinking about my past. Seven years earlier, I had graduated from Indiana University Northwest in Gary, Indiana, with a Business degree in Finance and Economics. I was lucky enough to interview and get a job right after graduation. The position was titled "purchasing clerk" at one of the two hospitals located in Gary. This position worked directly with medical vendors who shipped medical supplies and equipment to our warehouse or directly to the two free-standing hospitals located in Gary and Hobart, Indiana. The hospitals were thirteen miles apart. My main responsibility was to make sure that all medical supplies and equipment were available in the warehouse or storage areas when the patient care and support departments requested them. This position, while the pay was less than desirable, the responsibility of ensuring that the medical and nursing staff had what they needed to take care of their patients, gave me purpose.

It is now 6:00 am, and my son is dressed and ready for daycare. I'm in the mirror, making sure that my clothing is in place, my shoes feel comfortable (business pumps), and I have a knee-length lined skirt, so you can't see through it. My blouse had a round neckline, no cleavage showing, and the jacket fell just right at the top of my thigh, covering my rear end. I had no make-up on my face, just glasses, and my favorite shade of red lipstick.

Today is the most important career transition in my life. I worked hard for seven years, and it was finally paying off. My career in healthcare started as a purchasing clerk, promoted to Purchasing Manager, on to Assistant Director, and beginning today, my title was finally Director. I have got my new leather briefcase, a gift from my husband. Inside the case was my to-do list. I had a meeting with my boss (the Vice President) in his office, then other staff meetings that included department tours.

My first stop was daycare drop off. I kiss my son goodbye, and now it is off to my forty-five-minute drive to the hospital. Along the way, I thought about my conversation with my father, asking him, "Should I accept this new position in another town that I virtually know nothing about?" Through the years, I had heard my father and his older brother talk about our cousins, who lived in the city of my new employer. They would visit with them, and as a child, I remembered traveling there once with my mom's cousin and aunt to hear our other cousin, an opera singer, in concert. I had expected my father to say no to the hospital's offer. Surprisingly the answer was, "Yes, you have a cousin who works there as a security officer so you will not be alone."

I asked my father how I should get there. My father, who always went deer hunting every fall, said, "This is mating season, and there will be plenty of deer active day and night. The scenic route is slower and will give you more time to stop should deer cross your path." I took my father's advice and took the scenic route. The slower drive was pleasant and relaxing. It took my mind off worrying about the day ahead. The trees along the route were majestic, bursting with colorful leaves of red, green, and yellow. Some of the trees were so old and big that their limbs hung hundreds of feet high above my car and well over into the street.

I arrived at the hospital, where I was greeted by the front desk. I give them my name and the department name I wish to visit. The front desk attendant calls Administration, and my boss's secretary comes down and whisks me away to his office. My boss immediately welcomes me, we have small talk about our families, and then we move onto his view and vision of my areas of responsibility. He says he is thankful that I am here and ends our meeting, saying, "Good luck." His secretary picks me up from his office, gives me the schedule of the Monthly Directors and non-report departmental meetings I am expected to attend, and lastly informs me of the meetings I am responsible for chairing.

The Purchasing Manager, one of my direct reports, is called to escort me to my office. She arrives and we formally introduce ourselves to each other. She is an older lady who tells me she has worked at the hospital for more than 25 years. Along the way to my office, she tells me a little about each department that we pass and our current relationship with them. We finally arrive at my office, which is in the lower level with the other support areas, like Pharmacy, and my direct report areas: Central Service, Receiving, Purchasing, and Storeroom. The Purchasing Manager left me at my office door, leaving her card with her extension to call if I needed anything.

My new office was slightly larger than my old one. It kept an empty medium sized desk with lockable drawers, telephone, desktop computer, printer, filing cabinet, a chair, and two visitor chairs. I opened the drawers to find nothing in them, no minutes from meetings, no budgets, departmental goals, employee evaluations, or hospital department phone numbers. My predecessor, who had been in this office, left no trace of his existence behind. No one even muttered his name, out of respect, or maybe indifference.

Now it's lunchtime, and I am greeted by the acting Central Service Supervisor and Purchasing Manager, who invite me to lunch. I accept their invite and find the cafeteria has some great ham and navy bean soup. We have a lot of small talk about how long I have worked in healthcare, where did I live, what school did I attend, was I married, and did I have any kids...? I answered all their questions and asked the same of them. We went on to discuss our afternoon schedule of meetings. I would meet with Central Processing first since they started an early schedule beginning at 7:00 am. Afterward, I would meet with Purchasing and the storeroom personnel together, since they were smaller departments that worked the same schedule, 8:00 am until 4:30 pm. My last meeting would be returning to Central Processing to meet with the evening shift at 4:00 pm or so.

My first meeting with Central Service began at 1:00 pm. The acting supervisor introduced me to his staff, by name and title. I thanked him and then began to tell his staff about me, my overall healthcare experience, and my specific experience in Central Services. I asked that each staff member give me their name, the number of years working at the hospital, and lastly, what they loved most about it. The finale was the department tour. I felt that the meeting had gone well, and I was hopeful that they would all be that way.

My second meeting was with Purchasing and the storeroom staff. That meeting was going well; my introduction, my story, and the staff telling me who they were and what they loved most about working at the hospital. Now it was time for the departmental tour. They wanted to show me their inventory system and how it worked and were pleased to hear about new equipment like fax machines that had been implemented by other purchasing staff, making them more efficient. One more meeting had gone well, and I continued to be hopeful.

Now it was time to have my final department tour of the storeroom and the dock area. This is where all medical and operational supplies and equipment are brought into the hospital to be stored for later use or distributed directly to departments. The clerks were proud of their work area and showed me how they had organized the storeroom and their percent of complete orders. As I was ending my time with the storeroom staff, the lead storeroom clerk said, “The Hospital must be closing if you got the position.” I immediately asked, “Why do you think that?” “Well, there was another guy who interviewed for the position, and we never saw him again;” I explained to him that whenever there are open positions, generally there are at least three candidates interviewed. I was one of the last candidates to apply.

Now, I was beginning to silently wonder why I had not met any of the staff members before my first day? My mind began to question everything. I wondered how this 30ish white male who, beginning today, reported to me, felt so comfortable that he openly shouted out his presumption that at best, I could only get this position due to default. Had the thought of reporting to a Black woman and seeing me in the flesh overwhelmed him so much he could no longer hide his racists and sexist feelings. At that moment, there was no doubt in my mind he felt that a Black woman could not be the best candidate for the job. It wasn't me; it was my race and my gender. The fact that I had a Bachelor's degree in Business from IUN didn't matter. The fact that I had been responsible for the daily operations of two separate hospital's Materials Management areas 13 miles apart didn't matter. The fact that my performance evaluations were outstanding didn't matter. My seven years of hard work didn't matter. My three promotions in seven years didn't matter.

In his mind, a Black woman should not be allowed to perform at the Director level. For a fleeting moment, I felt betrayed, had all the staff smiling in my face, thought the same thing? Everyone sat there for several moments in shock. No one apologized that day. They just sat there wondering would his actions result in immediate dismissal. During the next two days, he reported off from work. I wondered about his feelings about the hospital's culture. To set my own barometer, I scheduled meetings with the other Department Directors to get a feel for management's culture.

I must say that I was pleasantly surprised at how warm, personable, and willing they seemed. Over the next few days, my staff began apologizing, saying he did not represent them. Upon his return to work, he admitted that his actions had ostracized him from all the other staff. We also talked about him being uncomfortable working at the hospital and whether he should seek employment elsewhere. He agreed, and within two weeks, he tendered his resignation.

While I was not happy with his outburst, it gave me a different perspective on race relations. My whole life, I had thought open racism occurred in the south. Every time we would travel to Mississippi, Mom and Dad would say, "THINGS ARE DIFFERENT in the south, you cannot eat in the restaurants, use their bathrooms, or drink their water. You are not to go anywhere by yourself." We were never told it was racism. It's just how things are down there. This experience opened my eyes that this type of direct open racism had no borders; it was in the hearts and souls of some all over this land.

I am yet hopeful that every human will one day realize the value of every man, woman, and child and begin to treat each other with respect.

About Deborah

Deborah Williford Simpson is a Mississippi born, Gary, Indiana raised, mother, grandmother, and caretaker living in the Indianapolis area.

She is currently semi-retired, a licensed insurance agent, and a substitute teacher. Over the last four decades, she has worked as the Director of Materials Management in various hospitals in Northwest Indiana and Chicagoland, as well as a marketing representative for various A-rated insurance companies.

She earned a Bachelor's Degree in Business, focusing on Finance and Economics from Indiana University Northwest. Ms. Simpson is a charter member of the Nu Eta Chapter of Delta Sigma Theta Sorority Inc. and a Golden Life Member. She is a Life Member of the IU Alumni Association and was previously selected by Outstanding Young Women of America.

Chapter 22
"Beauty Is…"

By Sonjia Pelton-Sam

Hello. It's me, The All American Church Girl. Can you relate? Many can.

My story, "Beauty Is," starts off like most stories from back-in-the-day. I was raised in a home that had both a mother and a father. I lived in a middle-class home with parents that did their best to shelter me from any and everything. I was a child who was very loving and full of fun. People often said that I never cried much as a baby. I was all smiles and coos. I was told that I was a child that could light up a room.

My mom worked very hard. She was a nurse who worked on the night shift. My dad often flew in and out of town on business trips. Instead of going to a nursery when I was a small child, my parents allowed me to stay with neighbors who were senior citizens, Mr. & Mrs. Mack, who were like my second parents. During the day, I would watch soap operas and drink coffee with them. I am still paying for all that caffeine today because I sometimes have the jitters.

As I remember back on those days, I must say that, for the most part, I had it good during my early childhood with Mr. & Mrs. Mack. They spoiled me. I could get up and move around whenever I wanted to. I took naps at my leisure and played with my toys at will. However, my transition from early childhood to school was difficult. At school, there was structure and order that I had to obey. My transition to school was very hard. There were some nice kids, but also many mean kids and bullies that I had to deal with.

It was during these early school days when I noticed that I was different. I had not noticed it before, but now my eyes were open to the fact. I saw that my skin was darker, and my lips were bigger than the other kids at my school. And there was also the matter of my hair. It did not look like the other kid's hair. Their hair was straight, and my hair was kinky. My hair would not lay down or stay down like the other kid's hair. I also noticed that the other kids had the whitest skin. I began asking, "Why can't my skin be white? Why can't I have straight flowing hair? Why is it that even though my hair is long, it is still not straight? Why is my hair stiff? Why am I unable to wind it into a ponytail? Why does my skin look like dirt?"

I was sad enough when I noticed my dark skin and big lips, and that I was different, but then it happened. One of the white kids asked me the Big Question: "Why won't your ponytails lay down? Why do they stick out?" Afterward, they all would start laughing. As I am now thinking back to that time, I don't think they were trying to be mean. I now realize that where they lived, they never saw a lot of little black girls.

Needless to say, during my time there, I made lots of friends, and from time to time, the same questions would come up. I learned to smile and overlook it. It was apparent that those that laughed at my appearance came from homes that did not teach acceptance of all races.

Life kept on rolling, and I finally made it to middle school. I found life to be much better in middle school. Middle school took me back to my roots. It was a breath of fresh air. The middle school allowed me to be me. I made new friends, and I was excited about school for the most part. My hair was no longer an issue because I saw more kids who looked like me. I saw puffy, bushy hair with no movement all over the place. I was happy.

However, it was strange that in a place where I found mirror images of myself, I still could hear the echo of laughing kids asking me about my HAIR!!! The echoes sounded so loud that it made me take action. It made me think of ways to solve the problem, and being the skilled, gifted, and talented person that God created me to be; I learned how to do my hair myself.

There was a beautician where my mom took me to get my hair done. Her name was Ms. Mattie. Ms. Mattie was ok, but she never made my hair bounce, fly, and flow in the wind as I wanted it to. I wanted the same hair my old friends had. I wanted "GOOD HAIR." During my 6th grade year, I started watching what Ms. Mattie was doing to my hair. I also watched the other beauticians and paid attention to how they styled their client's hair. I began practicing at home all of the different techniques I had seen.

On my birthdays and during the holidays, I started asking my mom if I could go to the beauty shops where some of the girls at my school went to get their hair done. It was hard to get my mom to say yes because she is one of those loyal-to-a-fault people. And if there were two things, she was loyal to, it was Church and Ms. Mattie. On a few occasions, I got my wish and was able to get my hair done at other beauty shops. When I did get my wish to go to the other beauty shops, I made sure I studied every beauty product on the counter. I observed every tool they used for each hairstyle. I noticed their every move – every twist of the wrist.

My hair was now starting to flow in the wind, but there was still one thing missing to make it take wings and fly. What was that one thing? What was that one missing piece to the hair puzzle? One day as I was getting my hair done, I saw the beautician pull out the missing piece: It was a jar of relaxer. That's right. It was a perm. I went home with my mind focused on that one thing: I begged and pleaded with my mom asking her to allow me to get a perm. She finally said YES. I found that "Perm" changed my life. I felt really happy, and my hair felt free.

I found that my life changed again when I moved from Fort Worth to Baytown, Texas. There, I experienced racism again, but more strongly. One day I was coming out of a local mall, and as I was walking to my car, a truckload of white men drove past. They began yelling out of the truck and called me a nigger. They laughed and drove off. My heart stopped for a minute. I had seen this type of straight-up racism on television, but I had never personally experienced it before.

My next experience with racism involved my son. He had a racist teacher. His teacher called and told me that my son had a lot of opinions and that he was a little too loud and vociferous. I asked her what she meant by that statement? When she explained what she meant, I concluded from our conversation that she expected him to be more subservient. She said she liked quiet leadership, as he was one of the student leaders in AVID. I explained that there could be no such thing as a quiet leader.

A few weeks later, the school had a big program that was run by this same teacher. She used my son as the main speaker. He practically ran the whole program by himself, and it was a huge success. At the end of the program, she passed out scholarships. She announced that she liked quiet leaders and gave scholarships to the other students who were white. My son was hurt. I told my son that from now on, she can get her quiet leaders to run the show. I will never allow anyone to use him and abuse him because of the color of his skin. He is a strong black man who has since earned a Master's Degree and is a leader in his company.

My words of wisdom to everyone are: "Always let your heartache become your next big break. Remember that God can use your 'misery' for your 'ministry.'"

About Sonjia

Sonjia Pelton-Sam, also known as "The GLAM Coach," is a wife, mother, and grandmother. Sonjia owned a successful business in Fort Worth, Texas, a salon that was the largest black-owned salon in the city of Fort Worth when it opened.

She is a National Speaker, former TV Show Host, Author, Mentor, and a Certified Life Coach who brings an abundance of excitement, power, and creativity wherever she goes. She holds an Associate of Arts, Associate of Arts & Science, & a Bachelor of Arts. She instructs those whom she teaches to have vision, clarity, and focus in all areas of life.

Chapter 23
"Scars from an Unfamiliar Womb"

By Tiffany A. Galloway-Foster

Civil Rights, as inferred by our constitution – guarantees equal social opportunities and equal protection under the law, regardless of race, religion, and other personal attributes. They include "The Right to Vote, The Right to a Fair Trial, The Right to Government Services, The Right to a Public Education and the Right to use Public Facilities."

I was born at the cup of justice reform at Fort Benning, Georgia, named after Henry L. Benning, a general who served in the Confederate States Army during the Civil War. The irony of it all is my father, an African American officer in the U.S. Army, met me for the very first time at a military hospital. It was on a base that celebrated confederate heroes who would have gagged at the very thought of my birth along with millions of other babies who were introduced to a world that had a stigma as to how it saw African Americans. Its eyesight only peered into a small "Black or White" lens. And there was no frame to hold an "in-between" lens, even for an infant whose blood dripped from both a white and black fountain….

My parents met and fell in love while my father was a student at Fisk University in the '60s. I know what you are thinking. You are getting goosebumps as I tell you about a "Love Story" … Two college students who fell madly in love…They studied together; they marched together; they protested together; and they fought together for equal rights. All is true, except for one minor detail. Although my dad was a student, my mother worked in the Administration Office at Fisk University. Only a few years younger than my father, my mother was described as woke before this word even became part of our "oh so deep" millennials' vocabulary.

My father continued his studies at Fisk University and graduated. With huge excitement, my great grandfather, great grandmother, and grandmother, along with other relatives, traveled to Nashville, Tennessee, from Gary, Indiana, to attend my father's graduation. After the congratulatory tears, hugs, kisses, and pictures, my father proudly introduced my family to a beautiful, intelligent, and striking young lady with blonde hair. Well, I guess I left out one other detail, my mother was really a brunette.

As *woke* as my mother believed that she was, it did not eradicate the fact that she and my father were from two very different worlds. The world of Black and the world of White. In 1967, the year that my father graduated from college, the Supreme Court ruled in the case, "Loving v. Virginia" as a precedent, that Virginia's anti-miscegenation law was in direct violation of the Equal Protection Clause of the United States Constitution. And it was that same year, that unknowingly my journey was set in motion. Two years later, my world would soon collide with their worlds; leaving a lasting imprint that would forever change my perception of race.

My father came from a strong religious background and what society would call "a good, Christian black family." Education was not foreign to my father. His grandparents attended Jackson State University, which was Jackson College at the time. Born to a sharecropper in the early 1900s in the thick of Jim Crow laws, my great grandfather pastored and built one of the greatest African American churches of his time. He continued to pastor that same church, take on leadership roles in the National Baptist Convention and was President of the Indiana State Baptist convention until his death in 1977.

Under my great grandfather's leadership, his church membership grew large in numbers and remained a beacon of light to the community. Whether his members were married with children or single parents, they were afforded the same love, hope, and grace. His members were politicians, educators, community leaders, parents, housewives, supervisors, business owners, bankers, homeowners, college students, janitors, and hard-working steel mills and factory workers.

Born in the 1920s, my father's mother graduated from high school at 16, received her Bachelor's from Jackson College, received her Masters' from Indiana University, and taught elementary school students. My father received his college degree, fought in Vietnam for our country, served as an Officer in the Army and received the Purple Heart because he was injured in the Vietnam War. Yet, my African American father could not step foot in my mother's home. My mother's Anglo-Saxon father would not allow his son-in-law to enter his home…simply because he was black. And no amount of education or pedigree would change my white grandfather's vision. Through his glasses, he saw my father as a nigger who thought too highly of himself…so highly of himself that my father mistakenly believed that he was good enough to marry his white daughter. I wish I could write this love story as a fairy tale, but that would not be the truth. The truth is, I never met my white grandparents, and no amount of DNA would ever change that.

My father grew from adolescence to adulthood under The Civil Rights Movement, a nearly two-decade struggle from 1954 to 1968 to end legal discrimination against African Americans. The Freedom Riders, organized by Fred Shuttleworth, in 1961, were brave young people throughout the country, black and white, who traveled throughout the South to test the Supreme Court's decision, which stated that it was illegal to enforce segregation laws for interstate passengers. Mobs of segregates mercilessly beat those brave riders, so much so that on May 21, 1961, Robert Kennedy, who was the U.S. Attorney General at that time, sent federal marshals to Montgomery, Alabama to help protect the riders and decrease the violence.

On August 28, 1963, a preacher and Civil Rights Leader by the name of Dr. Martin Luther King, Jr. delivered the famous "I Have a Dream" speech at the Lincoln Memorial in Washington, D.C. It was on that day that Dr. King reminded America that the Emancipation Proclamation, issued by President Abraham Lincoln on January 1, 1863, declared that "all persons held as slaves are and henceforward shall be free." He reminded America that the words of our constitution and the Declaration of Independence echoed that all men, black or white, are guaranteed the unalienable Rights of Life, Liberty, and the Pursuit of Happiness".

He also presented "a call for change" to the southern states, which continued to operate under the Jim Crow laws as well as the northern states who continued to provide unacceptable housing and practice job inequality under the auspices of freedom. Dr. King's dream, "that we will live in a nation where we would not be judged by the color of our skin but the content of our character…that black boys and black girls would be able to join hands with little white boys and white girls". Fifty-seven years later, African Americans are still fighting for equality. The economic and educational scales favor the rich and White America. And we have learned that although laws have changed, hearts have not. Those fears, prejudices, stereotypes, and perceptions are intact. And the African American male is perceived as Public Enemy #1.

In September of 63, Dr. King's speech appeared to be simply an illusion when four African-American girls lost their lives, and 14 others were hurt while attending Sunday School at the Sixteenth Street Baptist Church in Birmingham, Alabama…not by a natural disaster or explosion caused by faulty wiring, but by the racist hands of four Ku Klux Klan members who planted a bomb and killed innocent children without a sniffle or remorse. In fact, it would take 17 years from the date of this hate crime for justice to prevail.

On September 16, 1963, Dr. Martin Luther King held a press conference in Birmingham, Alabama, to speak out against the violent act and hate crimes that consumed Alabama and other southern states. President John F. Kennedy provided a national response in opposition to the recent act of hatred and admonished Alabama to awaken to the ongoing slaughter of African American people who were neither protected nor safe under the judicial system.

That same year, Alabama's Governor George Wallace sent police to four cities in Alabama to challenge our nation's federal order to allow African American children to attend school with Caucasian children. Thereby forcing President Kennedy to dispatch the National Guard to protect African

American children as they entered all-white schools for the very first time.

From the March on Selma to the King-led March in Chicago, the fight for equality for African Americans in the North and South weren't very different. Dr. King helped organize a peaceful protest to oppose housing discrimination in Chicago. An army of protesters made their voices known to bring equality to the United States by calling for local, state, and national leaders to enforce old laws and pass new laws, which would protect the freedom of every individual regardless of color, creed, or religion. My father watched intently as civil rights leaders such as Medgar Evers, Malcolm X, and Dr. Martin Luther King, Jr., sought to achieve equality along with a caravan of known and unsung heroes. In fact, my father briefly attended college in Indiana on a football scholarship before transferring to Fisk University. My dad was born in Mississippi and completed his secondary education in Northwest Indiana. But it was at an Indiana college where there were no Jim Crow laws that my dad endured the worst case of prejudice and racism.

On April 4, 1968, Dr. King was assassinated in Memphis, Tennessee. Mistakenly they believed that they killed a man on that day, but they could not silence his voice and lifelong work to achieve racial equality. His voice echoed even more triumphantly from the grave, and his work was not in vain.

Seven days later, on April 11, 1968, President Lyndon Johnson signed into law the Civil Rights Act.

My mother was a southern belle from Tennessee. In her world, they waived confederate flags and believed strongly in segregation. And the one forbidden sin she committed. She married a black man. I have two fond memories of my mother. One of those memories is a perfect picture of us on the beach. Why this memory is significant is because when my mother and father divorced, I was only two. I have pictures of my mother with me and with my father, but they are just that – pictures. I grew up without my white mother.

My father's family embraced me and overly compensated because my mother was no longer in my life. At the age of five, my father sat me down and explained that though my melanin was lighter, it did not change that I was an African American girl, and society would never give me a choice to choose. The beauty of my childhood is that my father never spoke ill of my mother. He assured me that she loved me. And, sometimes people make choices for themselves. Sometimes people make choices for others. However, at the end of the day, it's a choice.

I guess for me, I never felt blatant rejection from my mother. I felt, "Just Unfamiliar." Subconsciously, I had questions about her because she was still my mother. After all, she carried me for nine months and was a mother to me until she felt she could no longer be. Her reasoning for remaining estranged, I may never know. But I do know that if my father could not step foot in my white grandfather's house, she may have shielded me from a life of unnecessary rejection and pain from the DNA that was as much a part of me as I was.

As children, we learn the differences and similarities between black and white people. We are admonished and warned of what society is like, and what we should stay away from. I soon learned that what my father said to me was true. I am a proud, beautiful, intelligent black woman who is not ashamed of her heritage. I did not choose the womb that I was carried in, nor did I have a choice in the matter. But if I was ever going to heal and rise above my insecurities, I needed to choose not to equate my mother's abandonment with the color of my skin or me personally. Although my scars were hidden, there were still scars. And my biggest fear for my son was two-fold; dating a white woman and being targeted by the police. These are things that I drilled in him, sometimes to the point where my son became immune to the speeches. For me, the love story between a white woman and a black man ended when I was two.

It took me years to realize that my experiences were becoming a burden for not only me but my son. And though

I was physically present; I was making a choice for him like my mother made a choice for me. Yes, I needed to prepare him for the society that we live in, which he learned sooner than later. However, I did not have the right to write his Love Story and tell him who he could date or marry. I had to search deep within, and no longer allow my perception to keep me in a narrow space. I wanted to widen my eyesight and try on a different pair of lenses …that saw more than just black and white.

Prejudice and racism are just as real today as it was during my parents' era. We have made strides, but we have many more miles to go to ensure equality for all regardless of race, creed, color…For me, I did not want new scars from an old wound to surface. I did not want to carry around choices on my back that were never mine to make. Nor did I want to impose my choices on my son. For this to happen, I had to embrace my DNA. I had to become familiar with that part of me that seemed so distant. I had to own up to the fact that I am a product of a white mother and black father who, at one time, believed that their love would last until the end of time…That their Love Story was more powerful than any prejudice…that their Love Story was Bigger than any Bigot, regardless of where he or she may reside.

You see, I had to change my perception and view because I was sadly mistaken when I said earlier that my parents' love story ended when I was two. It was then that my parents gave me the freedom to love and enter the homes of relatives who wanted me there and whose love yet overwhelms me to this day. My story and the quest to right wrongs and fight for equality is still a fight for me, my son, and generations to come. It will get even better if we allow our children to love unconditionally and continue to fight prejudice without fear.

I have experienced my share of racism and prejudice…from both worlds. But, as I have gotten older and wiser, my mother's world and my father's world no longer collide…My mother has become familiar to me more now than ever…. And, my scars are simply reminders that I survived a Tale of Two Worlds….

About Tiffany

Born in Georgia and raised in Indiana, Tiffany A. Galloway-Foster is a Social Butterfly who found no problem taking root in Texas after graduating from high school. Ms. Tiffany, as she is affectionately called, soon became a Texan and developed long-lasting friendships that would prove to be Family.

Alumni of Indiana University and NAU, Tiffany used her background in speech, drama, music, fashion, Radio/TV, and journalism to mentor, teach, write and direct church and community plays. Growing up as a PK (Preacher's Kid), Tiffany is no stranger to the Arts, and walking into those roles was a natural transition that brought much joy.
At age six, she directed and wrote her first play, "The Little Lamb." From modeling to class president, from the debate team to acting, from singing in the choir to singing solos, from writing essays to writing plays, from planning programs to planning events, and from Dee Jaying to directing plays, Tiffany has always had a love for music, theater, fashion, and writing. Believing that she would follow a path of journalism and theater, Tiffany took a different journey that led to marriage and motherhood.

Although she would work in corporate America as an Executive Analyst for over 20 years, her passion for Event Planning, Designing, and the Arts never waned. And she devoted as much time to her passion as she did her career. Corporate America offered stability, but it did not eradicate her desire to fulfill what she always believed to be her true calling. Whether teaching or serving as Fine Arts Director at her church, Tiffany knows the value of providing a platform for all generations to come together for cultural, political, and educational enrichment as well as discuss the current issues facing our society.

Life's lessons and experiences challenged Tiffany to dream again. Event planning, designing, writing, and directing was never a side hustle or just a way to make extra money. It was and always will be a part of her very being. It was as essential to her life as breathing. "Transforming spaces, creating spaces, designing, and planning events that are chic and unique to every client," ...Before she could utter the words aloud, God heard her and placed the same desire in her dear friend and sister, Tammi. Thus, TiffEny's Signature, LLC, was born.

We were all created with unique qualities, which should be celebrated. Regardless of color, age, size, height, creed, or color, we all possess an inner beauty that makes us shine. Tiffany has always believed that "Fashion" should be the "exclusive to our inclusive." By creating designs to enhance our overall make-up and build, our "different" becomes our strength, and our strength becomes our Signature, and our Signature becomes our Style. Our style embodies our gifts, personality, and attitude. That is what makes TiffEny's Signature, LLC.

Tiffany has a strong and supportive family. She is also the proud mother of Trey, and godmother to many.

Chapter 24
"Handicapped Parking Citation Equals THIRD-DEGREE FELONY"

By Tamensia R. Nealy

It was a hot summer day, and I had one quick errand to run before heading to the office. All I had to do was take my mother to her doctor's appointment, which was walking distance from my office. Due to my mother's disability (she is legally blind), when possible, I try to park the vehicle in locations that are easy for her to identify. On this day, we decided that if she finished at the doctor before the end of my meeting, she would walk to the office and pick up the car to go shopping in the area.

As I have done on numerous occasions and locations, I parked the car in the handicapped position in front of the building, with the disability placard hanging from the rear-view mirror. My meeting ended early, and I went outside to see if my mother retrieved the vehicle, and she had not. As a result, I walked to the vehicle and noticed that there was a ticket on the vehicle. I thought it was strange because the placard was visibly hanging in the window. As I reviewed the citation, I realized that I placed the expired placard in the window, thus resulting in the citation for displaying an expired handicapped placard.

I picked up my mother, gave her the ticket, and said, "You must have picked up the incorrect placard." Typically, when something like this happens, the person who owns the vehicle (my mother is the primary and I am the secondary owner) and placard can plead not guilty, appear before the judge, explain what happened, show the correct placard, and the citation is dismissed. There was something strange about this citation. The citation displayed my name and driver's license information and my mother's address. This was strange because my mother is the primary owner, and the vehicle was registered at her address, not mine.

Approximately 30 days later, my mother appeared at court and spoke with the Judge, who directed her to see the Prosecuting Attorney, where she presented her current handicapped parking placard and driver's license. She explained that due to human error, the incorrect placard was placed in the window. The prosecuting attorney noted that the ticket was placed in my name as well, but that my mother's name is listed as the primary name on the vehicle and agreed to submit a motion to dismiss, as supported by House Bill 400.

The saga continues! Two months after appearing in court and receiving a dismissal, my mother received a call from a detective at the local police department. The detective stated that he was calling regarding a dismissed parking citation. The detective asked my mother to appear at the station for an interview regarding the dismissed citation, and my mother refused. She was in total disbelief that the local police department would want to question a tax-paying citizen about a dismissed citation.

My mother was so upset that she sent an email to her council representative, providing a detailed explanation of the events and copied the City Manager, Mayor, and Chief of Police. She never received a response or acknowledgment of receipt.

My mother was extremely concerned about the situation and why local law enforcement agents would want to interview her regarding a dismissed parking citation. My mother watches a lot of television shows centered around law enforcement and has a genuine concern for her safety and well-being. She did not want to end up in jail for a minor offense without merit. My mother was in total disbelief that local law enforcement was wasting tax-payer dollars, her dollars, on a baseless investigation, a parking ticket that was DISMISSED.

Ironically, during this ordeal, the local news was reporting on a story that pertained to nine officers who were terminated as a result of an investigation that lasted more than nine months. The terminations were due to the officers falsifying traffic reports to boost their performance reports. My mother began to see a disturbing pattern and became more uneasy about the precarious situation she found herself in because of a DISMISSED parking citation. She began to think about the possibility of becoming a victim of the same type of corruption at the hands of local law enforcement.

Unbeknown to her at the time that she was dealing with the harassing phone calls, detectives were questioning me as well about the situation. Unlike my mother, I was unable to simply hang up and refuse to talk to them because I am a municipal employee. My supervisor directly advised me that I was needed at the police department. No, this was not an unusual request, because I was the technical liaison for the Police Department.

I was escorted into a room by two detectives who began asking me questions about the day that I parked the car in the handicap area and about my regular lunch habits (I have no idea to this day why that was relevant). Now it is time for the "zinger," the main question---did I know a specific individual? I answered yes and stated that the person was a relative. The detectives finally explained to me that not only did I hang an expired handicap placard, but it also did not belong to my mother. It was my cousin's, who had visited a while back and had forgotten her placard. Yes, not only did my mother pick up the expired placard, it did not even belong to her. The Horror! How Could She Make Such an Error? I attempted to explain to the detectives how this was a simple mistake and that she does have a handicap placard issued in her name and that she presented it in court a few months prior to the special prosecutor. Crisis averted, right? WRONG!

The detectives continued to ask me additional questions, and it was at this time that I asked them if I was under arrest for placing the incorrect and expired placard in the window and that if I was not under arrest, this interrogation is over and I will see myself out. Of course, I phoned my mother immediately to discuss this troubling encounter, and we quickly realized that something was truly amiss.

Approximately two weeks after the interrogation, guess what showed up in the mail? Yes, the SAME citation, with a new number, arrived at my mother's house via certified mail. Approximately three days after receiving the revised citation, I hired a local traffic attorney to defend me in court. I found out that a court date was already set for exactly 30 days after the re-issuance of the revised citation. Nine days before my court date, my mother received a call from another local Sergeant advising her that there was a THIRD-DEGREE FELONY WARRANT issued for her arrest. The charge? "Tampering with physical evidence." Coincidentally, this was approximately one week after her email to the City council, Mayor and Chief of Police. Hindsight, the City representatives, in a sense, did respond to the email, she wrote – WITH A FELONY WARRANT. My mother phoned me immediately to advise me of the situation. I was mortified and in total disbelief! Thankfully, the officer was extremely helpful in offering guidance on how we should proceed to facilitate the process.

My mother contacted several attorneys and judicial acquaintances, seeking advice on the best course of action. As a result, she contacted a bail bondsman, and I had to drive my mother to the jail, resulting in her being booked into the system – fingerprints and a mugshot were taken. In my total devastation, as I sat in the car and waited for them to complete the booking process, tears began to form; I tried with everything in me to contain my emotions and be strong for my mom. That did not work; the more I tried, the harder it was. I took several deep breaths, through my tears, I talked to God and asked for guidance and strength, as this was a major storm developing in our lives. As I waited, cried, and talked to God, I experienced a rapid surge of emotions – anger, despair, self-pity, disgrace, uncertainty, joy, and strength. By the time my mother completed the booking process, God spoke to me, and at that moment, I was confident and prepared for the battle ahead, and it was time to put on that armor and get to work.

Speaking of work, I went back to work the next day to face a whole new set of challenges. My supervisor requested a meeting with me to let me know that I was being reassigned and would no longer represent the police department. Do you see how God works? He knew that the battle I was facing was going to be hard enough without the additional obstacle of having to smile in the face of my attempted oppressor daily. At that moment, I knew that was God speaking again and showing me that He already picked the battle that he wanted me to tackle, and He removed the distraction so that I could focus and emerge victoriously.

Approximately one month after charges were filed, my mother was advised that the arrest impacted her standing as a foster parent. The little boy that was placed in her home, and in the process of being adopted, would be removed from the home. My mother is a fighter and the strongest person that I know. Although friends and relatives advised her to just let the little boy go back into the system and focus on herself, this was not an option. I volunteered to take him into my home until the situation was resolved, but they would not allow him to live with me temporarily; my husband was not a licensed foster parent, although I was licensed and cared for the child regularly. The only alternative to ensure the best interest of the child was for my mother to eradicate herself from the residence and leave the child with her husband.

On top of everything else going on, my grandmother became ill, was hospitalized, and eventually transitioned. During this time, my mother was placed in a position to incur the role of caregiver for my grandmother. I watched helplessly, as my mother struggled to maintain her sanity and dignity, I did what I could to assist, but my mother is strong-willed and does not like to lean on anyone or feel as though she is a burden. As a result, she attempted to push me away, but I knew that her actions toward me were due to the circumstances and had no bearing on the love that she always showered upon me. Amid the chaos, my grandmother transitioned, and now we had to add the insurmountable task of planning her funeral. With the aid of friends and family that God so strategically placed in our lives, prayer, and His grace, we endured.

PRAISE REPORT! Five days after the transition of my grandmother, our attorney notified us that the county prosecutor dismissed the case, and it was not presented to a grand jury. Ten months of sleepless nights, tears, and feelings of despair, we did exactly what God said we would, we emerged victoriously.

As we neared the end of this situation, our attorney revealed to us that the judge who approved the warrant, which was presented to her by a white male officer, was an African American female and was the same judge who would hear my case regarding the citation. We later learned that this judge had a reputation for handing out harsher sentences to African Americans. My attorney advised me to pay the citation because the judge, who never heard from either defendant, believed the white male officer and decided that we were, in some way, trying to deceive the court.

According to a study published in the Journal of Quantitative Criminology (https://www.goodtherapy.org/blog/study-judges-may-sentence-black-defendants-more-harshly-0301161), Judges may sentence black defendants who commit low severity crimes more harshly than their white counterparts who commit the same crimes. I often wonder if the color of our skin was a factor in the officer's persistence and the affirmation of deception from the Judge.

As a result, I am more aware of racism/bias toward African Americans, from all classes of people and races. Bias is learned behavior, even for judges and officers. I do not know the burdens plaguing African American female Judges, but I do know that they are not immune to their biases against their race.

After a tumultuous ten months, my mother was reunited with her husband and adopted son. By no means will our lives ever be the same. We are constantly haunted by that treacherous year and have little trust in the judicial system, as we witnessed first-hand how racial bias and abuse of power can change your life forever.

About Tamensia

Tamensia R. Carathers Nealy is a Texas native who has been making waves and breaking stereotypes since she made her grand entrance in the world. Dancing to the beat of her own drum, she has never settled and is not afraid to voice her opinions or stand up for her principles.

Tammi, as she is affectionately called, has forged many new grounds without apology or regrets. Whether accepting a lead role in local production, singing in a major ensemble, or leading a team in corporate America, she has left an everlasting handprint to be admired and followed.

With her mom emphasizing education and serving as an example, Tammi received a Bachelor of Science degree in Business Management from Texas Woman's University, a Master's degree from the University of Phoenix in Human Resource Management and Project Management, and a Master's Certificate in Project Management from George Washington University. She is a member of IIBA (International Institute of Business Analysts), a member of PMI (Project Management Institute), and a member of NCL (National Charity League) – Fort Worth Trailblazers Chapter.

Although Tammi wears many hats and creating balance is tough, her love for children, her belief in equality (regardless of color, creed, or sex), and her zest for a promising future for generations to come are constant reminders that there is more work to be done. Donating her time or volunteering at her church, in her community, or for a charitable organization brings much joy despite a full calendar or hectic work schedule.

Tammi is currently the Chief Financial Officer and Managing Director for TiffEny's Signature. Every gift and lesson has prepared Tammi for her recent role as a business owner and CFO. She is not afraid to be different. She is not afraid of fashion. She is not afraid of competition. Moreover, she is not afraid to be a voice in a loud, crowded room. After all, there are still more bricks to build an empire.

There is nothing more precious than God and Family. Tammi is proud of her accomplishments, but she takes more pride in being a wife to Marcus Nealy and the mother of Braeden and Morgan.

Chapter 25
"The Color of the Law in America"

By Deloise Hill Moore

Color of Law is defined as any authority using his or her power to willfully deprive a person of any rights and privileges protected by the United States Constitution. It is designed to protect any person of their rights. Authority figures mandated to follow this law include police officers, judges, prosecutors, prison guards, mayors, city council members, congress, public servants, and other political figures. Breaking the Color of Law is a federal criminal offense. The offense is punishable by a range of imprisonment up to a life term or the death penalty, depending upon the circumstances of the crime under Title 18, U.S.C., Section 242. In 2012 there were 380 Color of Law civil rights cases. Some of the violations under the Color of Law are unlawfully confiscating property, falsely arresting a subject, falsifying records, use of cruel or unusual punishment to detain an individual, failure to keep a person from harm and attempt to kill. (United States Department of Justice 2020).

Because of the many police violations, living in constant fear became my reality. It was a reality chosen for me. The fear of not knowing if my children would return home safely at the ages of 10, 12, 13, 14 thru 18 by the hands of Police Officers that are sworn into office to protect and serve the community. These officers had the responsibility to obey the Color of Law, but they created a hostile, unsafe, fearful environment. My children were targeted, constantly harassed, stopped, frisked, and racially profiled. One of my sons became fearful of going outside (not unless I was with him) because of his constant encounters with the police. I would always be on high alert to keep an eye on my sons. My Los Angeles friends had already warned me of dealings with police when my children would become older. My thoughts were, do not make my sons fearful; this is not our reality. I was wrong; police brutality became my reality, moving forward in time.

In Orange County, CA, 2018, protests, marches, and rallies crowded the streets county-wide. Townhall meetings were called to give voice to the people. I remember very vividly at a town hall meeting, one of the questions posed by the panel was about *the talk*. The moderator addressed the audience, asking, "Do you know when to give *the talk*?" I thought to myself, and I pondered in my mind. *The talk*, what is *the talk*? Never would I have thought that *the talk* is the appropriate age a parent should have a conversation with their children to ensure they understand clearly if they have an encounter with a police officer, there is a high probability they may not make it home safely. They might even die. The panel moderator stated, while shaking his head, "By the age of 10". I thought, wow. Stunned, I looked around the room in disbelief with tears in my eyes, at the sea of faces that filled the room. The faces I stared at were city officials, judges, educators, sheriffs, district attorneys, mental health workers, police in uniform, clergy, psychiatrist, mothers, fathers, brothers, sisters, family, friends, and people from all walks of life. I could not believe what I heard. I was absolutely stunned and hurt that parents needed to talk to their young black males and put fear in their hearts at the tender age of their development when they were supposed to feel safe and secure. This fear factor imposed by a society of adults that are supposed to nurture, cultivate growth, and care for the child.

I am the mother of three sons. When my children were young, I always thought police brutality, social injustices, and inequality happened to other people like Rodney King, Fannie Lou Hamer, Natasha Harding, Martin Luther King, Medgar Evers, and in the inner cities and many others. Not realizing, I was born during the height of the civil rights movement and segregation in the Jim Crow South of Black Codes. The community I lived in was affected by the laws of systematic racism, put in place by a group of people to oppress another group of people, based on the Color of their skin and their economic status. Also, not realizing that one day, I would have to deal with racism on my front lawn and in my own home, resulting in a court case.

You know, they say, never call the police for anything. Once involved, they will arrest the people that called them and take them to jail. Well, this is what happened to my son and me. One beautiful evening (2016), I was walking down the street singing, happy, and meditating in my peace of mind. Unknowingly, I would turn the corner and soon encounter an experience that would forever change my whole life and my perspective of the justice system. The injustices that exist in the court proceeding and the police department to get a conviction is undeniable. It is one thing to hear about injustices done to another, but to experience injustice for yourself, for me, was unimaginable.

When the verdict came down as guilty, I could not believe what I heard; we had been framed. The room came to a standstill in slow motion and disbelief. I looked at the judge. I looked at the jury. I looked at the police. I looked at the attorneys, and the district attorney. I went into a state of shock. I began to scream. It was like I did not have a voice; I was powerless. I had been stripped of my dignity, standing they're numb, I was riddled in disbelief. I thought if they cannot hear my words, maybe they can hear my scream. I screamed, and I screamed, and I screamed, and I screamed. My son, sitting next to me, kept his composure. He said he would not allow them to break him.

My son and I never had the chance to tell the courts what had happened on that beautiful Sunday evening, the day the earth stood still. From our innocent perspective, we thought at least we would get a chance to tell our story to the judge and the jury. But during the court proceedings, the cards were stacked against us. The judge and court attorneys assured we did not have a jury of our peers. The jurors came from a lily-white community, thinking they had the answers for everyone else's life because they were privileged, had built their careers, and lived in affluent neighborhoods. They had convicted two innocent people because they did not understand how a court system operated. They did not understand that evidence could be tampered with and was not allowed in the exhibits. Also, the police officers have immunity. It is their duty to get a conviction, even if it meant destroying lives. Even the judge did not know the whole story. She based her decisions on incomplete evidence.

During the jury selection, I could see that most likely we would be prejudged, and it was highly likely the verdict would not be in our favor because the majority of the chosen jurors were clearly not of our peers, except for one. There was one person we were hoping that would stand in our favor during deliberation - a black man. During deliberation, he did vote in our favor. He was convinced to change his vote by the white jurors, particularly the lead juror, who told the judge of his decision. He stated there were not enough facts to prove the case. The judge asked them to go and deliberate further. In our case, the minds of the jurors were made up by the judge's proceedings, the police officers' false testimonies, false reports, and the attorney's faulty trial. We were convicted without telling our story or admitting the proper evidence to convince the jury of our innocence. It became a trial between two innocent people and police officers. It became a case, and not for the reasons we decided to have a jury trial. We just wanted to be heard. Only to find out, the court system does not work that way---where you could tell your side of the story to the judge or jury. The attorneys pick and choose what they want the jury and judge to hear. Judges can sway the decisions for or against the person being tried. The judge made sure we got individuals that had negative dealings with police officers or the court system. They knew they could create a story the jury would believe.

Even the District Attorney portrayed a hideous picture of me based on the lies the officers told. I did not even recognize he was talking about me. It was painful sitting there, listening to these white people tear my untarnished character to shreds. The evening of the travesty, I just wanted peace. I wanted everyone off my lawn, to go home, and leave us alone. But no, this gang of juveniles in police uniforms wanted to harass and terrorize us. It reminded me of an old black and white film I saw on television of the K.K.K. that kept harassing the blacks in their town. They beat this man and left him to die, just because they knew they could get away with it. These officers are trained to lie. They are trained to say, "I was fearful for my life," "he was reaching for my gun," and "stop resisting." Because this gives them the footing not to get a case. These officers have immunity: the court will protect them even if they are wrong. Under the Color of Law, probable cause and racial profiling give officers leverage to harass and target *particularly* black males. Just think of all the innocent individuals indicted for an offense that they never committed. Imagine being framed by a judge who was put in the position that is supposed to ensure that your due process rights are protected and that there is equal protection under the law. By the hands of the court system and police officers, our lives became a living nightmare. It hung in the balance of the unknown possible injustice one could pose on another.

I became fearful for my life and the life of my son. Due to my experience, I can feel the anguish and pain of the many others that had gone before me that were found guilty by a racist judge, a racist jury that was not of their peers, and racist District attorneys and public defenders. Also, evidence can be presented to the jury that can sway their decision.

This is what happened to us. The false testimonies, falsified reports, and partial evidence were presented to the jury to build a case against us. The judge must protect the public from harm. Clearly, the Judge, Prosecutors, Lawyers, and Officers violated the Color of Law.

Plea bargaining was the district attorney's initial offer of 2 years. Instead, we took our chances and went to trial, thinking we could tell the truth of what happened, and the case would be thrown out of court. Being coerced to plea bargain by District attorneys that are committed to criminal injustice will destroy a person's life. To win a case for notoriety, for promotion, and their own personal gain was out of the question. Many do accept a plea to ensure a lesser sentence, even though they are innocent. I know of a young man that was chased by some people at the park and apprehended by police. At the hearing, the head attorney tried to get him to take a plea of 8 years, she said, "You can get more time if you go to trial." He took his chances and represented his own case (Pro Per). The case was dismissed because the plaintiffs did not show up at court. Just think if he had taken the plea. I understand clearly now how the court system operates. Its mission is to ensure it gains as many convictions as possible. The court system is a faulty system that has too much power that can destroy lives and *has* destroyed many lives.

Getting back to the story… The police were called to my house to address a person with a mental health schizoaffective bipolar disorder. We thought we could help the person that had become irate. Screaming, hollering, spitting, and they had stripped naked, running into the street. When the police arrived, I invited officers to come inside my house. I was under the notion I could talk to the officers and let them know what had occurred. One officer was not interested in what I had to say and threatened to come back and kick in my door. I thought to myself, what did I invite into my house? I called my son on the phone to tell him the officers had made it to the house and to come, so we could tell them what had happened. When my son got to the house, the officer approached him and asked him to put his skateboard down, which was leaning against his leg, on the ground. When he put his skateboard down, the officers attacked him, knocking him on the ground. More officers came and began to beat him. One officer kicked him with his steel-toed boots and stomped him over and over again. Another officer was punching him repeatedly in his face. Officers were punching and kicking him in the head, in his back, and in the face, a countless number of times. I was screaming, "Stop, stop, stop, knock it off!" Absolutely disgusted and appalled, I was in disbelief this behavior was taking place. I was petrified and upset that my Sunday evening turned into chaos on my lawn.

Officers surrounded my son, and just watched the beating take place. They were beating him when he was already in handcuffs while they yelled, "Stop resisting, stop resisting, stop resisting!" Stop resisting, filled the air as screams of pain flowed from my son's mouth. Ten police cars were surrounding the house. Crowds of people gathered. I gained enough composure to begin recording. The police blocked my house and would not allow me to enter to use the bathroom. Finally, they beat my son until he passed out and placed him in the police car as though he were a dead animal. I stood there frozen, thinking---" Did they kill my son?"

I tried to reach my son, but the officers blocked me. They told me to stay back, using profanity. Other officers began walking towards me. I began to back up, fearful for my life. They snatched my cell phone from my hand and forcefully shoved me into the car, bumping my head. I felt I was being kidnapped. My thoughts were racing through my head, "What are they going to do to me?" I thought they would throw me into the river or take me somewhere to beat and kill me. I was terribly frightened, not knowing what they were going to do. The ride seemed forever; I was taken to the police station. When we arrived at the station, I noticed several of the officers were pacing nervously. I was thinking, "Did they kill my son? Where is my son?" Frantically, I asked the officers, "Where is my son?" I did not receive an answer. I was thrown into a cold cell for 6 hours. Finally, an officer came and said I was free to go home. He handed me my cell phone back, with a smile on his face, and stated, "We had to transport your son to the emergency room." When I got home, I checked my phone, just as I thought, most of the beating had been erased.

The hospital x-ray report stated my son had scar tissue in the nose and on his brain, bruises on his back, stomach, face, and arms, and his eye was swollen shut. Where they had purposely put the handcuffs on too tight, his hands were swollen.

The officers erased the footage of evidence that could tell a different story than the story that was posted in court. All the officers had turned off their Cam recorders, except the part when they were driving down the street. Ten police cars surrounding my house, the lawn was filled with officers, and no one had recorded the incident. Eight officers got together to fabricate a story to fit a scenario they made up to ensure they got a conviction against us. The only pictures exhibited at the hearing were the side of my son's face that did not show the injuries he suffered. They omitted the fact that they had beaten my son until he passed out and was taken to the emergency room. The Doctor's report was not put into evidence. They lied and stated I swung at a 6-foot officer, and he had to duck. I am only 5', 1". One officer busted out laughing because he knew he was making up his story as he was telling it.

NAACP members came to the proceedings. One member stated he would not believe it if he had not been in court to witness the court proceedings. He saw they had no evidence to convict us. I was convicted of interfering with an arrest. When, in fact, I was screaming, crying, and pleading for the beating to stop. I was fearful for my son's life. It was like watching the Rodney King beating. My son was convicted of resisting arrest and given six months in jail. An NAACP member was able to get me out of jail because my disabled son was sitting at the courthouse, waiting for the court to be over.

To bring about resolve regarding my case, and to increase awareness, I took measures to tell my story in 2016, when police brutality was at one of its highest, once again. I began to attend rallies, protests, and town hall meetings. Given every opportunity, I would speak about the injustices of America. I talked to the mayor, city council, and police chief. I filed complaints at the police department and filed a case against the city. I filed a claim with the appeals court. It was deemed not enough evidence, and the case was closed. My story fell on deaf ears with the city officials. At the end of a town hall meeting, a Black judge from Newport Beach approached me and stated that my story changed her view of judging cases. During this town hall meeting, a white lady yelled out that she wanted to know about mass incarceration. I proceeded to tell the mass of faces what mass incarceration is. Many had never heard about it.

Due to my experience, I can clearly see the reason so many Black males are locked up in the prison system. This system is designed to convict whomever they please because there are no checks and balances. America has 2.3 million people incarcerated, more than any other country in the world. The prison industrial complex is the New Jim Crow, it is modern slavery. Slavery did not end; it still exists in America. It just has a new name, Prisons for Profit. (Michelle Alexander, 2020). The prisons are paying inmates 23 cents per hour, which is pretty much free labor. Many companies use prison labor to make their products. For a list of those companies, go to www.mentalfloss.com. Private prisons turn over billions annually, according to the prison policy initiative.

There was a time in my life I had lost hope. I lived from a place of doom, gloom, fear, hopelessness, and despair because of outer social conditions. I had to realize that nothing outside of myself defines who I am—understanding that I am perfect, whole, and complete due to my divine birthright. The power lies within me, not within a system that is predicated on lies, deceit, hypocrisy, and destruction. Genius is my innate inheritance; this inheritance lies within each and every one of us.

Once I came into this knowledge, I became like a phoenix rising out of the ashes of despair, into my rebirth. I began to research, study, and learn about the human condition, from a historical perspective, and about mental and physical wellbeing. I also studied my D.N.A. family ancestry. I now understand the reason there is such a socio-political-economic divide. It became clear, understanding that the past affects the present. One must look to the past to understand who we are today. Historical events have a way of repeating themselves. According to the 2017 Kerner Commission report, it states that Black America is still at a disadvantage since the 1967 report, 63 years ago. Economist, Dr. Claude Anderson reports that Black people are going backward and have not progressed. He also states that Black people do not own a significant amount of anything to be able to control their lives. White America controls almost 100% of all the income, all the wealth, the power, the resources, and the business privileges in all levels of government that you cannot compete. He stated, "I am tired of hearing people telling Black folk, why do you not compete with Whites. What are blacks going to compete with?"

To see Systemic Racism in America, one must understand it is a social construct designed to deny systematic access to wealth and socio-economic-political stability. It is a system put in place to purposely deprive and marginalize another group of people and their human, civil, economic, and political rights. This system was put in place to create a society for whites only. This is the reason we have inequality today. Black Codes, Black Laws, Jim Crow Laws, and the K.K.K. were established to ensure inequalities remained in place.

Systemic Racism in America raises several questions such as, What Shall I do? Where do we go from here? Do I have a moral obligation? What are the principles of morality and ethical standards put in place by those that play a powerful role in establishing the fundamental guidelines of government officials and public servants? These laws were put in place by those that control the socio-economic structure of this nation. One principle that comes to mind is to do no harm, nonmaleficence. It states, "professionals have a responsibility to minimize risk for exploitation and practices that cause harm or have the potential to result in harm." (The APA.2010). Where have we gone wrong, America? How do we fix the problems of the Wealth gap, Prisons for profit, Mass incarceration, police brutality, the justice system, pipeline to prison, or the many other ills that have plagued this country since its inception, more than 401 years ago? America, for decades, has been in extreme violation of the constitutional rights of its citizens. We must take the necessary disciplinary actions and measures to correct our wrongs. There must be transformational change.

A shortlist of steps needed to bring about change:

1. Understanding that change starts with each individual
2. Research Black Scholars to aid in learning
3. We must create a new vision
4. Self-care
5. Push the candidates to make a change if they want our votes
6. Racial Wealth Gap is a serious problem
7. Boycott
8. Education Reform of the inner-city public-school system
9. Finance
10. Police Reform
11. Prison Reform
12. Carry a camera phone
13. Build our own entertainment industry
14. Accountability
15. Racial Profiling
16. We must continue in a national dialogue

Let us stand in Unity with one mind. Let us stand in solidarity. We are that which we are waiting for. Be that change. One nation of Love, Peace, and Harmony.

About Deloise

Deloise Hill Moore is a historian, community activist, actress, singer, and cultural event planner. Five of her great passions in her life are researching the history of various cultures, bringing awareness through cultural programs, advocating for those that cannot advocate for themselves, researching ancestral heritage and researching the effects of systemic racism (Jim Crow) in America.

She is a member of many organizations, attends educational historical seminars to continue learning about American ancestry. Has obtained certificates, and a Liberal Arts degree with a focus on sociology, anthropology, psychology, and theatre arts.

Some of her certifications and memberships are: Board Member of OC Mental Health Wellness Center, Member of NAACP, Member of National, Association for Equal Justice in America (NAEJA), Member of Learning Black History OC, Member of Be Well of OC/ Steering Committee of OC Mental

Health, Certified with National Alliance for Mental Ill (NAMI), Certified with Team Advocate for Special Kids (TASK),

Certified Specialist of Early Childhood Development, Certified Mental Health Worker, Certified Alcohol and Drug Studies, worked with No Child Left Behind, Member of O C Well Being Coalition.

Given Recognition from United States Congress House of Representatives Mental Health Association of Orange County, Student Recognition Awards for outstanding academic achievement of Saddleback College, Parks and Recreation of Orange County.

Currently, Deloise Moore is an event coordinator that specializes in teaching History through the vehicle of the arts of dance, singing and theatre at the O C Wellness Center, and in the community. She created the Mobile Museum that teaches History from a multicultural perspective. Also, she has lobbied the government in Sacramento, California for prison and mental health reform for policy changes. She is on the planning committee with O C Well Being Coalition of Mental Health.

Deloise Moore considers herself an intellectual. An intellectual that regularly breaks down old ideas, theories, and thoughts. She has learned to question the validity of all information. She is the person that asks why and seeks to learn and understand the current conditions of human existence. She believes in challenging all belief systems in understanding cultural evolution. She studies as far back as she can to understand and recognize the evolutionary process of all cultural values and belief systems that are relative to today. Who we are today is a sum total of our past experiences. We are still living the past events that have evolved into today's events of 2020.

She grew up in Southwest, Virginia in the Jim Crow South, attended a segregated school, and experienced school integration. Currently, she resides in Orange County, California.

Chapter 26
"Racial Injustice"

By Shantuan Coleman Taylor, PhD

I grew up in Cowtown, known as Fort Worth, Texas. Luckily, at the mere age of 5, my father gave me a quarter horse because he was a true cowboy. The gift of becoming an equestrian was one of many gifts bestowed upon me. My father's first encounter consisted of riding a horse named Little Colt, on our family farm in Mexia, Texas. My father's first two horses were named Trey and Shelia. The first-born colt was mine, and I named him Lucky. I grew up loving horses, trail rides, horse races, barrel racing, rodeos, and the Stockyards. The Fort Worth Stockyards is a National Historic District where the west began. Even today, I meet people of all races, born and raised in the Dallas/Fort Worth area, who do not know the Stockyards exist, or if they have heard of it, they have never visited. The Stockyards is the only place in the world where there are two daily cattle drives surrounded by historical tours, live music, 13 bars, 35 shops, over 17 attractions, and 14 restaurants. A few still serve authentic western cuisine.

My life consisted of horses, Math, and Science. I recall attending a different school every year, up until high school. I asked my mother, "Why did I go to so many schools?" She acknowledged my inquiry by saying, "It did not matter where you went, you adjusted easily, made friends quickly, and always maintained an A average. No harm, no foul, and you came out great!"

Growing up, I was a Jr. Princess in cowboy parades where I wore a sash and a crown. It set the framework for becoming a bougie cowgirl. I made being a cowgirl pretty upscale, even as a child. All my friends were afraid of horses until I met now Judge Raquel "Rocky" Jones as a child. She was the first of my friends that went horseback riding with me and loved it almost as much as I did. She has a winning personality, easy to talk to, and fun to be around. I remember the day we were playing with her Barbie Doll play pool, and we knocked it over. I quickly ran and got the vacuum. We were forbidden to use water in the pool, but as kids, we did anyway. We watched the water ooze from the pores of the vacuum bag. I ran and got a garbage bag and tape to catch the water. Next thing I know, I began to take the vacuum apart. I wanted to explore the science and engineering behind it.

Please sit back, kick your cowboy boots up, be careful with those spurs, and adjust your cowboy hat. Grab a cup of tea or a wine glass to get in a place of stillness and calmness as I share the discrimination I faced. There were three pivotal moments in my life that injustice by discrimination reared its ugly head. Here goes my story.

There was this diverse group of intelligent, high energy overachievers, often referred to as "Scholarly Magnet Students," that were bused to Dunbar High School and welcomed into the engineering program. It was located in the heart of Stop Six in Fort Worth at 5700 Ramey Ave. Many of you probably have seen the documentary called *5700 Ramey Ave,* which showcases the legendary Coach Robert Hughes' tenure at the school. He was coined as the longest winning high school basketball coach ever. After the documentary, the address 5700 Ramey Ave was later renamed Robert Hughes Way. The home of the Flying Wildcats. That honor was so befitting and touched my heart.

One of the highlights of my life was being a wildcat, alongside my father, while sharing the same alma mater. I attended one of his reunions, and he attended one of mine. The year we were going to attend an All Class Reunion together, he died just days before. I was devasted! I was a true Daddy's girl. I attended the reunion anyway. His Class of 1964 and my Class of 1987 welcomed and embraced me that night. They shared high school stories about him and his glory days of being a football player. I took it all in. I laughed hard, and I cried softly.

Pivotal Moment #1
Even at a Majority Black School, I was Not Shielded

My parents, Leroy and Doris Coleman, raised me to believe I could do anything I set my mind to accomplish.

Hence, one of my favorite quotes is by the 44th President, Barack Obama, paraphrased, "We can accomplish more than the art of science states is possible."

I remember that day like it was yesterday. My Algebra teacher was a slinky, medium height man who wore corduroys, whether it was winter, spring, or fall. He favored tan, light blue, and lime green shirts. On this particular day, he wore a light blue button-down shirt, brown corduroys pants, brown loafers, and had on a particularly shiny chain around his neck. He was a pale white man with a huge mustache that reached the end of his chin, and hair grew out of his ears. He had tiny beady brown eyes under bushy brows that appeared to be too close together. His face was adorned by these nerdy brown rim glasses and a fussy curly brown mullet style haircut. That day, I asked a couple of questions during his class to clarify a point. He had an agitated candor. Therefore, he blurted out in a matter of fact tone that I was incapable of learning math, and I would never be an engineer. I looked at him and said, "What?" He slyly stated, "You people can't pick up math easily." I think at that moment, I heard every single student in the class put their pencils down and join the conversation. Every race was represented in that room. I wasn't hurt, but I was truly pissed. I was confident, yet respectable, towards my teachers, and I always felt like he had a disdain attitude towards me. I always believed in myself regardless of the opinion of others.

All my life, I loved Math and Science, and I was good at it. I must admit his teaching strategy was erratic, in my opinion. As quickly as he wrote, he erased. Most often, he made me feel like he did not welcome inquisitive questions in his classroom. Once the bell rang, I vividly recall running as fast as I could down the hall, hearing Mr. Hicks and Mrs. Patterson asking me to stop running and slow down, and what had me in a hurry. I was angry, and I ran (all the way) to the principal's office. He was my middle school principal as well, so we were already acquainted. I sat down in a seat across from his desk, where his nameplate was gold with black lettering, and it read, Aubrey Peterson, Principal, with a wildcat mascot. He was on the phone and shuffling papers when I arrived. I asked if I could call my mother, and he insisted I tell him what happened. I said, "I want to be able to say this just once." He immediately stopped shuffling papers and told whoever was on the phone he had to call them back. He handed me the phone. I dialed my mother's work number and blurted out the whole story.

There were meetings and teacher conferences to address what had occurred. There was talk of firing him and moving me out of his class, but that was not the justice I wanted. I decided then and there I would become an engineer, and I needed him to remain so I could prove it.

After graduating with my Bachelor's in Electrical Engineering on Mother's Day, that following Monday, I drove up to the school, signed in, and asked to see Mr. Peterson. Access was granted. I popped into his office and gave him a big hug. He asked me what brought me back. I laughed out loud while stating, "Yesterday, I graduated with my Bachelor's in Engineering. So today is the day! It's Operation Back to Dunbar." Truth be told, I walked out of his office, thinking he did not have a clue what I was talking about at that moment.

I was escorted to my old Algebra teacher's classroom. Entering the classroom, I was warmly welcomed---surprisingly. I shared with him that I graduated from college yesterday and asked if it was ok to speak to his class, and he agreed. I think he remembered me as a previous student, but my name was met with a blank stare. He appeared not to recall, so I did not state it until I ended the purpose of my visit. I talked about my degree, the college experience, paid work internships, and my love for Dunbar and how the engineering program prepared me so well that I did not study very much during my first two years in college. This led me to share that teachers will have either a positive or negative impact on your learning, whether short-lived or life-long learning.

I shared how I sat in that very classroom, humiliated, as I was told what I was incapable of achieving. I told the students not to allow anyone to dictate what they can or cannot accomplish. I thanked the teacher for allowing me to speak as I began to share what happened to me. I decided that I would not be a victim; I would not entertain victim language. I emphasized that I was a creator, and I utilized creator language and actions. "I stand before you as a degreed engineer. My experience in this classroom was very impactful. It was a negative experience that changed the trajectory of my life in a powerfully positive way."

While ending my story and speaking passionately about my encounter in that very same classroom, I stated, "I am..." Then in unison, Mr. Peterson and my old Algebra teacher said my name aloud, "Shantuan Coleman." At that moment, I had just realized that Mr. Peterson knew exactly why I appeared that day, and in that instance, my old Algebra teacher remembered my name. He jumped up and interjected, "I never said or spoke those words to you or any student." I took a deep breath and calmly stated, "Yes, you did. Why else would I be here sharing my story?" I said boldly, "Don't you ever say that to another student!" I proudly walked out of his classroom after laying a framed degree that stated in bold letters, Shantuan Antoinette Coleman earned a Bachelor of Science in Electrical Engineering, and I said, "This is to ensure you will never forget my name again."

Pivotal Moment #2
Being an Exception Within Your Race

I constantly heard engineering was a male-dominated field. I did not feel the impact because I kept looking around in my college classes, and numerous times, I counted the male vs. female ratio, which was almost equal. Hence, it was just a myth to me. All I saw were female students that looked just like me. Blame it on being at a Historically Black College or University (HBCU), but I would not have wanted anything different than an HBCU experience. Looking back, every school I attended prior to high school, with the exception of Dunbar Middle School, was a predominately white public or white private school. After receiving all my college prospects, I had narrowed it down to 3 schools. Prairie View A&M University (PVAMU), Texas A&M University (TAMU), and Southern University (SU).

This little bougie cowgirl wanted a small country college town that produced and boasted high numbers in graduating engineers that looked like me---talked like me. At that point, it was down to economics, and PVAMU cost my parents the least amount of money with the scholarships. Also, I could still participate in all things cowboy by attending PVAMU. Not to mention, the city has a rich history of trail rides and cowboys. I fell in love with the beautifully landscaped institution of higher learning. I totally felt safe and secure at PVAMU and when traveling through both cities of Waller and Hempstead, Texas. PVAMU was smack dead in the middle of both cities, which were only a few miles apart. I road my horse on several back roads and through fields, not to mention drove my car down most of Waller's roads.

My nieces followed in my footsteps and attended Prairie View A&M University just less than ten years previous to the Sandra Bland's case, where she was taken into custody for a traffic misdemeanor and was found hanging in a cell, which became public knowledge and swept the nation in 2015. Just imagine the fear and deep concern for the plight of people of color that swept through me. Knowing that I was once headed to pick up one of my own nieces at that same Waller County jail cell for a misdemeanor, but she was released before I arrived.

After graduating, although I was an electrical engineer, I convinced my newest employer that I could do the job of a civil engineer. During this time, I had an interracial relationship with a Vietnamese engineer who had just graduated from TAMU. Initially, it started as just co-workers going to lunch in workgroups whenever socially asked by other colleagues. Then we started avoiding group luncheons and opted for just going to lunch together, which led to our first date. We went to the circus. Don't laugh; we were only recent graduates straight out of college. Hence the circus scene had not lost its appeal at that time. It was a safe date diversely attended.

My Asian boyfriend was very attractive, well-liked, dressed well, and drove an eye-catching red sports car. He was the perfect gentleman, very attentive, and a lot of fun. Every member of his immediate family, including the husbands and wives, lived in the same house. It was a large stately house in a predominately white neighborhood. There were enough rooms for everyone. Eight people lived in his home. He owned a car wash, laundry mat, and moonlighted as an engineer by day. They all collectively ran two beauty supply stores and their own businesses that were all located in black neighborhoods. They equally supported each other's businesses without complaint. I thought it was phenomenal that they all lived, worked, and pulled together.

As a couple, we did everything together. We introduced each other to various new things, such as cuisine, attractions, places, religion, and our cultures. He was a Buddhist by family tradition, and he did it more so out of respect for his ancestors and parents, and less for himself. I am a non-denominational Christian because I am a believer and do it because I like it without a family obligation attached. Being unevenly yoked never affected the relationship beyond an occasional weekday contractional *prayer play date*, as I affectionally referred to them as when it landed on a day that I wanted us to attend an event. He began to skip a prayer play date or two, upon my request. Our dates consisted of him taking me to all things Asian, and I took pride in exposing him to all things Black. We both respected our differences and gained an ah-ha moment about our differences that we both embraced. We were the perfect "blackanamese" couple.

We covertly planned lunch dates, never taking the elevator at the same time, and meeting in the garage to head out for lunch. And once there were rumors that we may be dating due to our daily lunch dates, we opted for taking separate cars, and cryptic conversations over the phone and in public to quieten the office talk. This led to more evening dates to remove suspicion. After he casually asked me to be his girlfriend, he shared that he no longer wanted to hide our relationship from our colleagues. My friends and family had all met him and genuinely liked him. I had spoken to his siblings and met his youngest sister. I conceded to going public with our relationship. It had been well over a year at that point.

Once revealed, most of our co-workers accepted us as a couple, with the exception of an Asian female, who had a huge crush on him and often shared with me that Asians typically, do not date outside of their original race. For example, Vietnamese only dated/married Vietnamese, and Cambodians only dated/married Cambodians. We spoke about our shared lives and respected cultures that we both merged.

One day, Mi, his sister, asked how he felt in the midst of all the black people/culture I had exposed him to. At that moment, I thought to myself; no one has ever asked me how I feel amidst a lot of whites or Asians. I waited for his response, and he proudly stated my friends and I were different. I was puzzled, so I had follow-up questions. He went on to say how I was educated and well respected, as well as the friends I had introduced to him. So, I asked what other types of black people he had been exposed to in his life. I needed to get a handle on his perspective and quick. I asked him how the black students at Texas A&M were, and he stated he did not have any black friends in college. So, I asked then, what other blacks was he referencing in terms of differences? He was digging a hole, but I listened intently. He said I was an exception to my race. I stopped in my tracks and exclaimed, "What? How so?" He paused and appeared to be searching for words that would not offend me. I asked why Mi seemed to be comfortable with asking how he felt amidst black people. He said she meant different from the blacks in the hood that frequented their business.

I swallowed hard and took a deep breath as I asked him to describe the blacks from the hood that frequented their family business. Oddly enough, he did not seem perplexed until he noticed the look of disdain on my face. He asked, "Are you ok?" and "Did I say something that upset you?" He further explained that he would never do anything to hurt me intentionally, and I believed him, but I was still mad as hell.

At that moment, I realized something new about him and how it would change us. He never meant any disrespect. He just was not cognizant of how he expressed himself as it related to the blacks. The night ended with my saying goodnight before I said something I might regret. He went in for a goodnight kiss, but I met him with a cheek. He left without saying another word. A week went by, and I avoided him at work and ignored his calls. He sent flowers with a card that read, "I do not know what I did that caused you to stop talking to me, but if you tell me, I promise I will never do it again!" Signed "Love-n-Stuff," a sign off I use when ending my notes. I think I borrowed that from one of my favorite childhood authors Judy Blume or Beverly Cleary. I silently chuckled at the note. He knew every nuance about me but did not realize that he could not love me and despise my race at the same time.

I asked my secretary to take the flowers over to his office where a wall of elevators and five floors separated us. He grabbed the note that read, "The love we both get! It's the "stuff" that you are failing miserably," followed by asking, "Is there a reason why I have never been invited to your house or met your parents?" My secretary came back with the following observation: "He appeared frustrated when he noticed I was returning the flowers. Then he dropped his head in anguish after reading the card."

He came to my office. His face was red, flushed with emotion. He closed the door and exclaimed, “Enough!” He went to a conference room on the 7th floor and said, "Meet me there in 5 minutes." I had never seen him frustrated or angry before. I arrived in the conference room, which had no windows, and the lights were bright. He grabbed my hands and shared that he enjoyed the life we created, spending all our time at my condo. I never thought, not coming to his house would be an issue for me or us. He told me that he had never brought anyone home to meet his parents. Followed by, a black person has never stepped foot in their house in his entire life. He just blurted out the answer to my question written on the card. Something I knew but never thought the concept affected us because of our relationship. He reminded me that Vietnamese traditionally only date Vietnamese. "My parents would never approve of our relationship," he said. And that is why I was never invited to their house. I reacted like a detective by asking questions. "You mean, your parents are not aware that I am black?" He said that they were aware I was black. I peered at him, and he said, "What they don't know is that you are my girlfriend." My mouth fell open." He blurted out, "They think you are a co-worker; I just never updated them on our relationship status."

Not until our recent conversations did I realize, unintentionally, he appeared racist, explaining my race, due to his parents' influence of actually being racist.

That year the movie "Jason's Lyric" came out starring Jada Pickett Smith and Allen Payne. We went to see it. We discussed the movie. I asked him what the movie was about. He stated, "Violence. It was just black on black crime." I swiftly started asking him SAT prep like questions about the movie, something he could relate to, and share an honest opinion. The first being about the premise of the movie. I asked would he say the movie was based on man vs. man or man vs. nature. He answered, "Man against man." I became annoyed as I explained how it was man vs. nature. The true subtleties of our differences began to unravel, and even if we never knew it before, we could no longer pretend it did not exist. He and I broke up until he thought he could share our relationship status with his parents. It took longer than I had planned to wait. Seeing him daily was difficult, so I landed a job at NASA Johnson Space Center.

Pivotal Moment #3
Hitting the Glass Door Even in Space

There was a sense of accomplishment working at NASA. As a payload engineer working on the International Space Station, I was responsible for the project management of Crew Systems and the Habitability module. My job on the project was to update the technical review boards, which were equivalent to presenting a safety and error-proof system that could withstand the atmospheric pressure of space travel. It was the job of those review boards to poke holes in the design and functionality of the projects. It was like facing a firing squad, and their sole purpose was to massacre you. Coming out of that board room unscathed was like getting an Olympic gold medal. If you failed, your reputation was at stake, and your job in jeopardy. It was exhilarating, rewarding, and stressful all at the same time. I was under a lot of pressure. I created action plans to prioritize problem resolution and technical issues. In addition, part of my job was to document planning and procedure activities for various electrical teams. I used every skillset and systems management tool I have ever learned and still conducted research to be in a position of certainty because lives depended upon it.

Once while working with the Russians, I was paired with a stately older white male engineer with a mechanical engineering background. I had a translator to assist with communication for the project workload. Although we had consistently talked through translated software without incident, he apparently never had a clue that I was a young black female engineer. Racism crept in the moment he laid eyes upon me, just like in the "Hidden Figures" movie. Instantly he had mistaken me for a secretary and requested coffee, which was a non-issue for me. I had begun to locate the coffee area and started asking how to make coffee. I joked that I did not know how to make coffee, and neither did I drink it. In hindsight, I quickly learned that jokes are difficult to translate and should be avoided because the funny part often gets lost in the translation. At that time, our translator chimed in to explain I was his engineering counterpart, and it was not in my job description to serve coffee. The language barrier shielded me from realizing how upset he became. Russian, in my opinion, was a harshly spoken language where every word sounded angry even though I was in the process of learning the language.

We typically received a dossier on our engineering international counterparts that do not reveal race or gender to date. I still wonder why? Was it widely assumed that all engineers were white males, or was it to prevent a level of discrimination? Although it was explained to him that getting coffee was a courtesy not within my job description, he remained steadfast that he needed coffee, and as a woman, I should know how to make coffee regardless. If only Starbucks locations were around, things would have been simplified. He later shared with me that he had a daughter older than me, and he could not believe I was actually his engineering counterpart. The following day he offered an apology, and we readily got back to work without further incidents.

To be honest, it was a huge learning curve, emotionally, mentally, and professionally. I quickly recalled the statement that engineering is a predominately white male profession. No matter how often I looked around at this point in my career, there were fewer women and even fewer that looked like me. It was apparent that the ratio that I had become accustomed to at my HBCU was fading quickly.

I shared pieces of my life, where I just wanted to pick up the phone and ask my parents how to proceed, how to respond, and how to feel…? I wasn't prepared for that kind of racism as a teen, but I held my own. I was becoming into my own. Meaning it was time for me to start becoming me. Of course, I used what my parents instilled in me, but I was never prepared for what was to come, and actually, who is?

We are living in the past with an updated flare. Everything that is really is not as it appears. What should be more valuable to you? Figure that out quick. Right now, today, we are teaching our teens how to respond when an officer pulls them over. It is imperative to share the do's and don'ts to remain alive after police pull you over just because your skin has melanin. Simply just because the color of our skin is black.

In hindsight, I would have handled each of these situations differently as a resolve. My teacher used a subtle overture, "You People," instead of saying "black" to downplay what he *really* wanted to say. Yet, I knew exactly what he was trying to say. I wish I would have thought to ask, "Since you choose to teach Math at a predominately black school and strongly believe that blacks can't comprehend math concepts, why not just fill the need and create better strategies for the black population of students you teach, to comprehend those concepts? Just take the time to combat the issue instead of enabling the minds of the students that are here to learn. The answer is easy; creator language needs to be taught at home and school in the primary years as a parent and during elementary school as a teacher. Avoid victim language at all costs. According to the University of Maine, Academic, and Advising department, creator language sends a message that there is always room to improve and do things better. Creators seek opportunities to change their behavior, whereas victims stick with the behavior and continue to get the same negative results. As a professor, I taught a course called EDUC 1300, where I used a textbook authored by Skip Downing. He discusses how victims focus on their weaknesses while creators focus on how to improve by using more positive language. Victims make excuses, and everything is based on or because of someone else. Creators seek solutions and always figure out what they can do to improve in an area. In addition, it should be taught to the teachers as an in-service as well.

Now to the blackanamese encounter, I am not sure that a resolution is required here, but I just wish I would have had patience with the relationship. Patience is truly a virtue, and I simply did not apply it here. I knew, without a doubt, he loved the ground I walked upon. My life experiences allowed me to gravitate to my insecurities of being at predominately white private schools and being the only Black that represented my entire race without my permission. Having to speak for my race in elementary and middle school was too big of a burden when I just wanted to hula hoop, do Mad Libs, read the Right On Magazine, and be the fastest kid to solve math problems. I never wanted to be an exception to my race. I just wanted to have a positive impact on it. It reminds me of 50 Cent's bold lyrics that state, "I want 'em to love me like they love Pac," referring to Tupac. However, I would say, "I want 'em to love me like they love Michelle, as in Michelle Obama. I need that from my race, not outside my race.

Glass ceilings will always appear; each and every one will handle them differently based on their maturity and the tools they inherited based on their life experiences. Never allow anyone to stop your "go!" I hit a glass ceiling early in my career. I was just excited about reaching it. There is not enough information out there that tells you how to break it. Be fearless, be bold, be creative, strategic, and productive. Just be "you" yet move in silence.

All three of these pivotal moments experienced allowed the realization that there are times in your life where you run into subtle racism. Whether in the workplace or at play, as well as within educational institutions. Some choose to ignore it. I, on the other hand, choose to face them head-on while remaining cognizant and respectful. It becomes a teaching moment, an area for cultural exploration and, in some cases, advancement. Life is full of experiences that will shape your character and moral being. Attack it with grace and poise to effectively deal with stereotypes, ignorance, and all the unknowns. Be the change agent to educate versus giving in to the negative connotations in which we are trying to dispel. Today we live in a climate where subtle racism is no longer hidden but used overtly and intentional since voting in #45. Engage cautiously and effectively…yet stay woke.

About Dr. Shantaun

Dr. Shantuan Coleman Taylor is a cowgirl from Fort Worth Texas. She is an engineer, professor, entrepreneur, STEM advocate, Chief Financial Officer for DTN Network TV, and author with a writing focus on non-fiction. She is affectionally known as Dr. Shantuan.

Dr. Shantuan has written several books, "I have a PhD: Now What", "Simple Little Words: Huge Impact", "Sticky Note Journal for the Busy Woman", and "How to Make Money Moves".

Dr. Shantuan is a contributing writer for the Melanin Family Magazine. She is also a fledging scholar who has written technical white papers for NASA, universities, and for conferences. As a serial entrepreneur, she created the Home Staging Lens – an interior designing firm, founded Brown Girl Empire – dedicated to empowering women and where she advocates for those whose lives have been impacted by uterine fibroids and started TaylorConvos – where she discusses concepts that affect us daily.

Dr. Shantuan is a lifetime member of the National Society of Black Engineers (NSBE) where she created STEM programs for pre-college and collegiate scholars. Dr. Shantuan is a member of Delta Sigma Theta Sorority, Inc., and Who's Who of International Professionals.

In addition, she is an avid passionate international speaker and sits on several boards. She is an equestrian that loves riding horses, trail rides, and teaching Sunday School. Dr. Shantuan is currently living in the Dallas/Fort Worth area.

Find out more at:

www.drshantuan.com

https://www.facebook.com/shantuan.colemantaylor

https://www.facebook.com/browngirlempire

https://www.instagram.com/browngirlempire

Chapter 27
"Mama to the Rescue"

By Yolanda Johnson Bailey

The resounding voice that came blaring from the classroom door was very familiar. At the back of a third-grade teacher's classroom sat a bushy ponytailed little girl, at her small wooden desk. Never did she expect to see the face that had just appeared before her, in what seemed like the blink of an eye. It was like one of those scenes from the television sitcom "Bewitched." One minute the doorway was empty, and the next, a silhouette appeared. The little girl was minding her business (if she had any at that young age) and was in a relatively good mood, but within seconds, all that changed. The atmosphere completely shifted when the little girl's mama showed up at her classroom door. She was unannounced and obviously agitated.

To her, this was new. Thoughts dashed through her little mind at full speed. Her mama had never shown up at her school before, mainly because she was not a student that got involved in any type of mischief. She knew if she did, it would land her "...in a world of trouble", as her mama would say. So, she did her work as assigned, respected adults, followed the rules, and did not bother anyone. Yet, she possessed a fear on this day that trouble may have finally sought her out. As her mama crossed the threshold of the doorway and entered the classroom, she began an exchange of words with the teacher. It was apparent this conversation was not warm and fuzzy. Her mama's voice started to escalate. The teacher's face slowly turned from a neutral skin tone to a warm shade of pink. Then in an instant, her mama had taken the reigns of the classroom into her authority. Like that of a military sergeant, she loudly demanded, "MOVE HER BACK...AND I MEAN PUT HER BACK RIGHT NOW!"

The little girl was nervous. She knew she could feel safe because her mama was present, but she wasn't accustomed to seeing her this livid. There were never any arguments in her home. Her parents got along exceptionally well. She was not around people who lost their tempers, so this was foreign behavior. On pins and needles, she didn't know what to expect. Was a fight about to break out? Then, she was summoned to the front of the classroom. "Oh no, I'm really in big trouble now." she thought. Figuratively speaking, she was shaking in her boots. That frightened and confused little girl was...yep, you guessed it. She---was---me!

Now let me fill you in on what happened the day before. It was a typical morning with my routine of getting dressed for school and meeting up with my neighborhood friends to walk to the bus stop. I grew up in what was considered the hood. For whatever reason, the kids in our neighborhood were bused to the other side of town to a predominantly white school for the third through fifth grades. I was somewhat excited about seeing my new school. The day I jumped off that yellow school bus and entered the halls of Bruce Shulkey Elementary marked the beginning of a new chapter in my life.

For me, not only did I have to adjust to being bused to the other side of town. Out of all the black students from my neighborhood, I was the only one in magnet classes (currently known as honors classes). I am sure you can imagine how uncomfortable and intimidated I must have felt. It was indeed an honor to be considered an advanced student. I know my parents were as proud as a peacock showing off its beautiful feathers, but I was not sure how I felt about being separated from the friends I was familiar with.

Ok, back to the details. I arrived at school and took my seat as usual. I cannot vividly recall whether we could choose the desk we wanted to sit in. All I know is I was front and center on the front row of the classroom. The day was going as usual, when out of nowhere, my teacher told me to gather my things and go to the back of the classroom. I did exactly as I was told while wondering what I had done wrong. Usually, when a student was sent to the back of the classroom, it was due to some type of behavioral issues. That was not the case here; therefore, I could not fathom the reasoning for my unexpected move to the back row. No other students were switched—only me.

My third-grade teacher was a middle-aged white lady with a very stern look on her face. The last white teacher I had was Mrs. House. Mrs. House was terrific. She was always nice and caring and never made me feel like some little black girl that she didn't want in her presence. I looked forward to each day in her class. She even invited her husband to the school to meet her six-year-old students, like we were VIP. I remember it like it was yesterday. Happy House---that was his name, and it described him to a tee. These were two of the most pleasant people I had ever met. If only I could say that about my third-grade teacher.

The evening came of the same day I was moved to the back of the classroom. Unlike the modern-day way of eating on the go, my family always sat down together at the dinner table. Either my mother asked how my day went, or I volunteered to tell her. I don't remember which way it went, but she found out that my teacher moved me for what seemed to be no apparent reason. I knew, without a doubt, this was serious when Mama paid my teacher a visit the next day. Looking back on that moment, I have no clue how she even made her way to the school. My daddy worked a full-time job, and we only had one vehicle, but somehow, she made it, and boy did she mean business. Within minutes, I was moved back to the front row, to sit in the desk I originally had before all "you know what" broke loose.

Of course, the naivety of the 6-year-old me did not understand what I had just experienced was an act of racism. You may be reading this and thinking to yourself that it wasn't a big deal. What I would say in response to that thought is, what I experienced, may be considered minor, but I refuse to downplay it. It's time out for that. And we never know how traumatic a negative experience can be for another person. In my case, I had a loving and concerned mother who intervened on my behalf. Not all children have that. I can't help to think what may have happened next, had my mother not immediately (and literally) confronted racism in its face. When I say literally, Mrs. Johnson had her finger all in that teacher's face. I think she may have even touched her on the nose. She was serious about her child not being mistreated…that was for sure.

I look back on that day and thank God that the outcome was not different for her. What if the police had been called on her for defending me? What if, like so many innocent children, I would have witnessed my mother being handcuffed, beaten, arrested, or even killed? I know it sounds extreme, but this has been the reality for some Blacks. Performing our normal daily activities can somehow turn into complete nightmares. The living rooms of our homes can quickly become crime scenes, with our own dead bodies as part of the evidence. We can be doing absolutely, positively nothing wrong at all, but simply---living while black.

That's precisely what happened to my father while driving home from work one day. This was back in the 1970s, and I was probably around 7 or 8 years old if I had to guess. Daddy drove trucks for a warehouse. He was headed home after a long day at work, and while enroute, his car was hit.

Thankfully he was okay, but not his Chevy Malibu. It was completely totaled. I realize accidents happen, but when I heard my dad explaining to my mom how these two young white guys were the ones who hit him, and how they were boisterously laughing and mocking him, it made me sad. I've always looked up to my father. In my eyes (and like most little girls), he has always been my hero. So, to hear how he'd been disrespected was a bummer. I felt deflated. Daddy never bothered anybody. He's the kindest man I know. He was minding his business and going about his day when trouble came lurking. I am not 100% sure that those guys hit my dad's car because he was a black man, but in my heart, I believe race played a part.

A few days ago, I ran across a video clip of a conversation taking place between four men. Two of them were black, and two of them were white. The dialogue they were having was about racism within the body of Christ. It was extremely intriguing, and one of those types of conversations that, if you're flipping through channels, you can't help but stop and listen to what's being said. One of those men was Dr. Tony Evans and another one of those men was Pastor Robert Morris. This was a very candid conversation taking place, and I could appreciate the transparency of Pastor Robert Morris, as he shared how he'd had some thoughts about Blacks that he was not proud of. He went on to tell how God has changed his heart and his mindset, and now he teaches other white pastors and preachers the importance of taking the lead on this racial issue and addressing it from their pulpits. As they conversed, Dr. Tony Evans spoke these words, "When you have unaddressed prejudice married to power, you're going to have an unintended pregnancy that will give birth to an evil baby called Racism." All I could say was, "Wow!" That was deep!

This statement couldn't bear to hold any more truth. Prejudice has gone unaddressed for years and years. In our schools, in our homes, on our jobs, and even in our churches. Mainly our white churches. I whole-heartedly agree that this is an excellent place to start addressing this monster of a problem. If more white churches teach about agape love and true equality for ALL, I'm crazy enough to believe we would witness positive change. I think the attempts to cultivate peace would not be interchanged with hostility.

It makes me think about my third-grade teacher again. What was she taught? We all know a person's background or upbringing has everything to do with how their character develops. Maybe she was raised in a racist environment. Perhaps that was all she knew. Just like it was new for me to be in a classroom full of white students, it may have been just as new to her, having a black student on her roster. Even if that were the case, it still doesn't justify her actions.

My being sent to the back of the classroom is no different than my mother being sent to the back of the city bus because she wasn't good enough to ride up front. Or her being sent to the back of the restaurant to order food because Blacks couldn't walk in the front door of an eating establishment and order from the menu, and they definitely couldn't have a seat at the counter without facing pure hell. There is a myriad of black women and their family members who have suffered racial injustices, and they have been minimized or altogether forgotten as if it's of non-importance. Some have been drastic, like the beating, lynching, and murder of multitudinous black people in America.

On the other hand, some have been more quiet and subtle. Not on display for all to take notice, but still happening. We have made the grave mistake of discounting the small acts of racism. I have learned that sometimes little things have huge impacts. An act of racism is still an act of racism, whether big or small, whether committed toward someone old or someone young. It doesn't matter a person's financial status or religious views. Racism is racism. When small acts are ignored, we allow them to grow into massive dilemmas that cannot be contained, very much like we are witnessing today. As blacks, we felt like Dr. Martin Luther King put us on the right path toward equality and liberty.

Fifty plus years later, we see that the freedom we thought we had has been somewhat of an illusion. The issues of racial injustice have escalated across our country like deadly cancer rapidly spreads throughout a person's body.

I refuse to lose hope for people of color and will hold fast to the thought that one day we will indeed be seen and valued for the amazing people God created us to be.

I pray we will not be judged because of the race we were born into.

I pray no parent receives a detrimental phone call regarding their black sons, grandsons, or other family members.

I pray we respond to hatred with love.

I pray that a genuine desire to become more educated and aware sweeps across our nation.

I pray that the people of this world will come together and unite as one human race.

I pray we find a way to end racism so that its gripping jaws can never hurt or harm another black person in America again.

I pray we look to God for guidance.

I fervently pray…for change.

About Yolanda

Yolanda Johnson Bailey, also known as Yolanda FaithEyes, made her grand entrance into the world on

October 11, 1971, in Fort Worth, Texas. Yolanda grew up in a spiritual home and is the fifth of six children. As the daughter of a church deacon, she learned about Jesus and was heavily involved in church ministry from a small child. Yolanda graduated from Paul Laurence Dunbar High School and later studied business at Tarrant County College and the University of Phoenix. She also obtained her certification as an Inspirational Life Coach through the Xcellence Leadership University.

Yolanda FaithEyes is an author, singer, speaker, and playwright. She is the self-published author of “My Children Are Gay & They’re Still My Blessing.” Despite the many challenges in life, Yolanda's singing is what kept her grounded. She released her first solo project, “All About Love,” in 2014. Yolanda uses her life experiences and opportunities as a guest panelist and speaker to help encourage, uplift, and financially bless other women. She has been the featured guest on the Let’s Godsip Podcast, STEM Radio Show, Sandra Reyna Stanley Ministries Talk Show, and The Talk of Life Talk Show With Elma. She has also been featured in the Fort Worth Black News, Voyage Dallas Magazine, and Girlfriends Gathering Magazine.

Yolanda is the founder of Faith Eyes Inc., a 501(c)(3) non-profit organization with a vision for all women to see themselves as special (because they are), beautiful (because God says so), and victorious (because they can be by faith). Faith Eyes Inc. provides charity giving and spiritual support through its programs.

Yolanda loves spending time with her family, especially her children and her adorable g-babies. She calls them her "Too Live Crew." Yolanda's compassion for people is undeniable, and her mission is to touch lives by spreading the love of God while sharing her gifts unselfishly.

For more information, or to follow Yolanda on social media, please visit:

www.yolandafaitheyes.com
www.faitheyes.org
Facebook - Yolanda FaithEyes Bailey
Instagram - @yolanda_faitheyes

Your Chapter

Your Title: ____________________

Now, it is time for you to speak out. Use this space to outline YOUR story of racial injustice in America!

Hope

My hope is built on nothing less

than Jesus' blood and righteousness.

I dare not trust the sweetest frame,

but wholly lean on Jesus' name.

On Christ, the solid rock, I stand.

all other ground is sinking sand.

Edward Mote

What is hope? It is apparent, according to the meaning given by Merriam-Webster, HOPE is something black women have gripped tightly as far back as we can remember. Our HOPE is our desire with the expectation of obtainment or fulfillment. It is what we want to happen, expecting it with high confidence.

On our darkest days, it is our HOPE that has kept us optimistic about a bright future and an expected end. As the painful residue of racial injustice infiltrates our nation, it is our HOPE that love prevails and our prayer that miraculous healing sweeps through our cities.

We possess a HOPE that our stories will encourage other black women also to speak out. We HOPE people of other races will become more enlightened by our truths.

As mothers and grandmothers, our HOPE never dies.

As sisters and friends, we keep HOPE alive.

It's in God our Creator

Our HOPE ultimately lies.

Our HOPE is built on the assurance that God will never leave us, nor will He ever abandon us.

He is our strength.

He is our peace.

He is our refuge.

He--- is our HOPE!

God's Word On The Matter...

SUFFERING

And the God of all grace, who called you to his eternal glory in Christ, after you have suffered a little while, will himself restore you and make you strong, firm and steadfast. 1 Peter 5:10

Praise be to the God and Father of our Lord Jesus Christ, the Father of compassion and the God of all comfort, who comforts us in all our troubles, so that we can comfort those in any trouble with the comfort we ourselves receive from God. 2 Corinthians 1:3-4

Not only so, but we also glory in our sufferings, because we know that suffering produces perseverance; perseverance, character; and character, hope. Romans 5: 3-4

I consider that our present sufferings are not worth comparing with the glory that will be revealed in us. Romans 8:18

The righteous person may have many troubles, but the Lord delivers him from them all. Psalm 34:19

ANGER

The Lord is gracious and compassionate, slow to anger and rich in love. Psalm 145:8

In your anger do not sin. Do not let the sun go down while you are still angry, and do not give the devil a foothold. Ephesians 4:26-27

My dear brothers and sisters, take note of this: Everyone should be quick to listen, slow to speak and slow to become angry. James 1:19

Do not be overcome by evil, but overcome evil with good. Romans 12:21

But now you must also rid yourselves of all such things as these: anger, rage, malice, slander, and filthy language from your lips. Colossians 3:8

ENEMIES

The Lord helps them and delivers them; he delivers them from the wicked and saves them, because they take refuge in him. Psalm 37:40

No weapon forged against you will prevail, and you will refute every tongue that accuses you. This is the heritage of the servants of the Lord, and this is their vindication from me, declares the Lord. Isaiah 54:17

The highway of the upright avoids evil; those who guard their ways preserve their lives. Proverbs 16:7

For in the day of trouble he will keep me safe in his dwelling; he will hide me in the shelter of his sacred tent and set me high upon a rock. Then my head will be exalted above the enemies who surround me; at his sacred tent I will sacrifice with shouts of joy; I will sing and make music to the Lord. Psalm 27:5-6

That we should be saved from our enemies, and from the hand of all that hate us.

Luke 1:71

FORGIVENESS

Be kind and compassionate to one another, forgiving each other, just as in Christ God forgave you. Ephesians 4:32

For if you forgive other people when they sin against you, your heavenly Father will also forgive you. Matthew 6:14

Bear with each other and forgive one another if any of you has a grievance against someone. Forgive as the Lord forgave you. Colossians 3:13

Do not judge, and you will not be judged. Do not condemn, and you will not be condemned. Forgive, and you will be forgiven. Luke 6:37

Then Peter came to Jesus and asked, “Lord, how many times shall I forgive my brother or sister who sins against me? Up to seven times?" Jesus answered, "I tell you, not seven times, but seventy-seven times." Matthew 18:21-22

LOVE

Love is patient, love is kind. It does not envy, it does not boast, it is not proud. It does not dishonor others, it is not self-seeking, it is not easily angered, it keeps no record of wrongs. 1 Corinthians 13:4-5

And over all these virtues put on love, which binds them all together in perfect unity. Colossians 3:14

Let love and faithfulness never leave you; bind them around your neck, write them on the tablet of your heart. Then you will win favor and a good name in the sight of God and man. Proverbs 3:3-4

Be completely humble and gentle; be patient, bearing with one another in love. Ephesians 4:2

And now these three remain: faith, hope and love. But the greatest of these is love.
1 Corinthians 13:13

HOPE

Be strong and take heart, all you who hope in the Lord. Psalm 31:24

Praise be to the God and Father of our Lord Jesus Christ! In his great mercy he has given us new birth into a living hope through the resurrection of Jesus Christ from the dead. 1 Peter 1:3

For I know the plans I have for you, declares the Lord, plans to prosper you and not to harm you, plans to give you hope and a future. Jeremiah 29:11

Why, my soul, are you downcast? Why so disturbed within me? Put your hope in God, for I will yet praise him, my Savior and my God. Psalm 42:11

But those who hope in the Lord will renew their strength. They will soar on wings like eagles; they will run and not grow weary; they will walk and not be faint. Isaiah 40:31

Made in the USA
Coppell, TX
04 November 2020